Colin Chapman

CHRISTIANITY ON TRIAL

BOOK THREE

Questions about Jesus Christ

Lion Publishing

CONTENTS

EXPLANATION OF SYMBOLS

Introducing each of the seven questions dealt with in the three books

A road intersection sign then shows the various possible answers

Each answer is then introduced by this route sign

Two further symbols appear within the answer sections:

A one-way sign points out the effect or consequences of a particular answer

A hazard sign shows the problems or questions arising out of the answer

LION PUBLISHING
PO Box 50, Berkhamsted, Herts

First edition 1974
ISBN 0 85648 028 2
Copyright © 1974 Lion Publishing

Printed in Great Britain by Compton Printing Ltd., Aylesbury, Bucks

ILLUSTRATIONS

Acknowledgements

Lion Publishing, pictures on pages 10, 12, 19, 36, 42, 43, 52, 55, 69, 85, 86, 87, 95, 108, 110; *Camera Press*, pages 13, 15, 21, 24, 25, 28, 32, 38, 39, 47, 51, 60, 61, 65, 74, 113, 121; *British Museum*, page 37; *Buzz Magazine*, page 73; *Warner Brothers Ltd.*, page 78.

GENERAL INTRODUCTION

'I could tell you my adventures – beginning from this morning,' said Alice a little timidly: 'but it's no use going back to yesterday, because I was a different person then.'

'Explain all that,' said the Mock Turtle.

'No, no! The adventures first,' said the Gryphon in an impatient tone: 'explanations take such a dreadful time.'

Explanations take such a dreadful time. But if we omit them, we are likely to meet with this reaction:

'What *is* the use of repeating all that stuff,' the Mock Turtle interrupted, 'if you don't explain it as you go on? It's by far the most confusing thing *I* ever heard!'

Is Christianity *true* or is it not?

How can we possibly *know* whether it is true or not?

These are the basic questions before us in putting Christianity on trial. We are dealing primarily with Christian beliefs about God and Jesus Christ, about man and the universe. We are asking whether they tell us 'the truth' about ourselves and about the universe in which we live.

But how can Christian beliefs be put on trial?

Questions about Jesus Christ

There was a time when it seemed very simple to prove the truth of Christianity. A Christian could stage a trial which ended like this:

Judge: Gentlemen of the Jury, I have laid before you the Substance of what has been said on both Sides. You are now to consider of it, and give your Verdict.

Foreman: My Lord, we are ready to give our Verdict.

Judge: Are you all agreed?

Jury: Yes.

Judge: Who shall speak for you?

Jury: Our Foreman.

Judge: What say you? Are the Apostles guilty of giving false Evidence in the Case of the Resurrection of Jesus, or not guilty?

Foreman: Not guilty.

This happened in England in 1729.

Recently a similar trial was staged in a youth club in Scotland, but with significant differences. This time a Christian was put on trial, and the charges against him were these:
1. that your faith is based on a myth – the resurrection;
2. that your faith is irrelevant to life in the twentieth century.

All who took part in this trial were speaking for themselves and expressing their own beliefs; they were not acting a part. A few were Christians, but most were not. The audience were the jury, but there was no vote at the end. The judge in his summing up simply explained that each person must decide for himself whether or not he thought the Christian was guilty on these two charges.

If the idea of this second trial appeals to you, or at least makes some sense to you, you may want to go straight to the third book in this series, which deals with the evidence for Jesus Christ, the meaning of his death and the question of his resurrection.

Questions about God, man and the universe

To many, however, this second trial will sound just as strange or absurd as the first. If you cannot understand or accept Christian beliefs about Jesus, it may be because you do not accept some of the most fundamental Christian assumptions about God and man and the universe, and not simply because you are not convinced by the evidence about Jesus.

Bishop Butler, writing in 1736:

It has come, I know not how, to be taken for granted, by many persons, that Christianity is not so much a subject for enquiry but that it is, now at length, discovered to be fictitious. And accordingly they treat it as if in the present age this were an agreed point among all people of discernment, and nothing remained, but to set it up as a principal subject of mirth and ridicule, as it were by way of reprisals, for its having so long interrupted the pleasures of the world.

J. S. Mill:

I am ... one of the very few examples, in this country, of one who has not thrown off religious belief, but never had it: I grew up in a negative state with regard to it. I looked upon the modern exactly as I did upon the ancient religion, as something which in no way concerned me.

Nietzsche, writing in 1865 at the age of 21:

If Christianity means belief in a historical person or event, I have nothing to do with it. But if it means the need for salvation, then I can treasure it.

Mahatma Ghandi:

I may say that I have never been interested in an historical Jesus. I should not care if it was proved by someone that the man called Jesus never lived, and that what was narrated in the Gospels was a figment of the writer's imagination. For the Sermon on the Mount would still be true for me.

Colin Wilson:

The need for God I could understand, and the need for religion; I could even sympathize with the devotees like Suso or St. Francis, who weave fantasies around the Cross, the nails and all the other traditional symbols. But ultimately I could not accept the need for redemption by a Saviour. To pin down the idea of salvation to one point in time seemed to me a naive kind of anthropomorphism.

If, therefore, your questions and objections about Christianity are about fundamental assumptions about God, man and the universe, there will be little point in making Jesus the starting-point of the discussion. You ought to begin with one or more of the questions in the second book in this series. Who or what is 'God'? Does 'he' exist? What is man? Who am I? What kind of universe do we live in?

Questions about definition and truth

But what if you are not sure what Christianity is?

James Mitchell:

I used to be a convinced Christian: I am no longer a convinced Christian: I am no longer convinced. In fact like many others of my generation I am profoundly uncertain as to what 'being a Christian' actually means any more.

C. E. M. Joad:

If you will forgive me for mixing my metaphors, to criticize Christianity is like assaulting a feather bed with the consistency of a jelly and the colours of a chameleon.

And what if the idea of putting *any* ideas or beliefs on trial sounds absurd?

The hero in Henri Barbusse's novel L'Enfer:

As to philosophical discussions, they seem to me altogether meaningless. *Nothing can be tested, nothing verified.* Truth – what do they mean by it?

Michael Harrington:

The contemporary spiritual crisis is the result of this simultaneous loss of faith and anti-faith ... Its unique characteristic is that no one really seems to believe in anything.

C. E. M. Joad writing about the war of 1914–18:

Then came the war ... When it came to the point, the ethics of Christianity were, it seemed, as incapable of practical application as its history and biology of scientific verification. The whole religion as it is taught and preached today thus came to seem a gigantic swindle ...

Margaret Cole:

It is partly because I care for verification that I cannot believe in any 'revealed religion' ... When the question of the *truth* of Christianity was raised in my mind ... I perceived almost immediately that it was not true, and that it could not possibly be proved to be true; and the burden of religious belief fell from my back as easily as did the burden of Christian in *The Pilgrim's Progress*, and has never shown any sign of returning to its perch.

If you share these feelings, or have a strong sympathy with those who feel this way, you will probably have to begin with the questions about definition and truth in the first book in this series.

The method and material used

Each of the main sections (in the case of Book One, the whole book) has an introduction outlining the general approach and defining the question being tackled.

Then the 'road intersection' shows the possible answers to the question.

Each answer is then examined in detail.

Much of the book consists of quotations from different writers, because it is important that we should try to feel the full force of what they are saying. Where there is merely a summary of a person's position, the summary is in most cases taken from a writer who has no particular axe to grind or does not share the outlook of this book (for this reason much use has been made of, for example, Paul Hazard's books *The European Mind 1680–1715* and *European Thought in the Eighteenth Century*). Where italics have been used they are the italics of the original author.

Quotations have been chosen from the philosophers, tracing the history and progression of their thought; from the arts, because often this is the area where beliefs can be worked out and carried to their logical conclusions; from other religions, because East and West are becoming more aware of each other's ways of thinking and no approach to Christianity should leave them out of account; and from modern theology which has been profoundly affected by the history of ideas.

Finally, some problems and questions about the Christian answers are dealt with.

The starting-point

What is 'Christianity'? There are so many definitions that it is necessary, before we begin, to say something about the starting-point of this book.

There are three possible ways of answering the question:

Try to find the lowest common denominator in all the different definitions of Christianity that are offered; limit the definition to include only those items which all Christians or the vast majority of Christians would accept without question. ,

Refuse to define Christianity at all. Allow each person to have his own understanding of Christianity, and show the maximum tolerance towards anything which is described as 'Christian'.

State your own understanding of what Christianity is, at least as a starting-point; further discussion will show to what extent it is consistent with the mind of Christ.

This third approach is the one I have adopted. I shall take as my starting-point what is generally called Biblical Christianity; *i.e.* dependent solely on what we know of God and Christ from the basic documents of the Bible, both Old and New Testaments. This understanding of Christianity is not that of any one church or denomination.

No discussion is held from a purely 'neutral' position. Therefore the aim in stating my own position is not to be sectarian and doctrinaire, but simply to declare the book's starting-point openly and clearly.

The position of this book, then, is basically a committed one. But its method is open. It is for the reader to start where he will, at the point where he is. He can examine the options, follow up which he wants in the order he wants. It may mean going back to an earlier question to be settled first.

Then it is for the reader to make up his own mind, to follow up the evidence – and act accordingly.

Living with your beliefs

It is not enough simply to outline different answers and consider them coldly as possible theories for discussion. We have to ask: *what does it feel like* to live with a belief about God, to go through life with a particular understanding of man, or to live in one kind of universe?

For this reason the quotations (including those from the Bible) are intended, not simply to convey the answers in a theoretical way, but to help us enter into the experience of those who hold these particular beliefs.

We follow up the different answers to see where they lead, applying the 'simple but profound test of fact': i.e. '*does this concept really work; do its consequences fit our experience?*' (Bronowski, see BOOK ONE, p. 21). In each case we need to ask questions such as these:

— what would happen if we were to be thoroughly consistent and take this belief to its logical conclusion?

— what would happen if we were to live as if this belief were really true?

And for '*what would happen if . . .?*' we can usually substitute '*what has happened when . . .?*'—because there have always been people who have tried to be consistent in their search for the truth, and have explored all the possible answers and their consequences.

In many cases we shall discover what Francis Schaeffer calls the 'point of tension' between what a person believes and the real world in which he has to live. If a belief leads to disastrous consequences, or if we can only hold it by not being totally consistent, then it is highly likely that our belief is not true. We are then faced with a choice:

either we accept the full consequences of what we believe

or we look for a different belief which stands up better to the test of truth.

A change of mind of this kind is bound to have a profound effect on all our attitudes. If Christianity is true—and if we are prepared to consider this possibility—we have to be willing to change our minds, to open them to the truth which God has revealed, and see where this leads us. This process of change involves the heart and will as much as the intellect. Jesus said: 'Whoever has the will to do the will of God shall know whether my teaching comes from him or is merely my own.'

QUESTION FIVE

"What was Jesus' relationship to God?"

If we can assume that Jesus was a real historical figure, was he anything more than an ordinary man? If he was related to God in some special way, how are we to describe this relationship? The main evidence we have to consider in the four Gospel accounts concerns his birth, his character, his claims about himself, and his miracles.

HIS BIRTH

Two of the Gospels begin with an account of the birth of Jesus. His birth is described as a perfectly natural birth, but his conception as the work of the Holy Spirit.

Matthew describes the events from the point of view of *Joseph*, who was at this time engaged to Mary:

Now the birth of Jesus Christ took place in this way. When his mother had been betrothed to Joseph, before they came together she was found to be with child of the Holy Spirit; and her husband Joseph, being a just man and unwilling to put her to shame, resolved to divorce her quietly. But as he considered this, behold, an angel of the Lord appeared to him in a dream, saying, 'Joseph, son of David, do not fear to take Mary your wife, for that which is conceived in her is of the Holy Spirit; she will bear a son, and you shall call his name Jesus, for he will save his people from their sins.' . . . When Joseph awoke from sleep, he did as the angel of the Lord commanded him; he took his wife, but knew her not until she had borne a son; and he called his name Jesus.

Luke describes the events from the point of view of *Mary*:

In the sixth month the angel Gabriel was sent from God to a city of Galilee named Nazareth, to a virgin betrothed to a man whose name was Joseph, of the house of David; and the virgin's name was Mary. And he came to her and said, 'Hail, O favoured one, the Lord is with you! . . . Do not be afraid, Mary, for you have found favour with God. And behold, you will conceive in your womb and bear a son, and you shall call his name Jesus . . .' And Mary said to the angel, 'How can this be, since I have no husband?' And the angel said to her, 'The Holy Spirit will come upon you, and the power of the Most High will overshadow you; therefore the child to be born will be called holy, the Son of God.'

HIS CHARACTER

There are at least four features which stand out clearly: compassion and anger, humility and goodness.

Compassion

Jesus' compassion shows in his attitude towards the crowds:

They went away in the boat to a lonely place by themselves. Now many saw them going, and knew them, and they ran there on foot from all the towns, and got there ahead of them. As he landed he saw a great throng, and *he had compassion on them*, because they were like sheep without a shepherd; and he began to teach them many things.

—towards children:

They were bringing children to him, that he

An inscription with the name of the Roman Emperor Augustus, who gave the decree for the census that took Mary and Joseph to Bethlehem. Bethlehem was David's home-town, the prophesied birth-place of the Messiah.

might touch them; and the disciples rebuked them. But when Jesus saw it he was indignant, and said to them, 'Let the children come to me, do not hinder them; for to such belongs the kingdom of God . . .' And he took them in his arms and blessed them, laying his hands upon them.

—towards the sick:

And a leper came to him beseeching him, and kneeling said to him, 'If you will, you can make me clean.' *Moved with pity*, he stretched out his hand and touched him, and said to him, 'I will; be clean.' And immediately the leprosy left him and he was made clean.

—towards the bereaved:

As he drew near to the gate of the city, behold, a man who had died was being carried out, the only son of his mother, and she was a widow; and a large crowd from the city was with her. And when the Lord saw her, *he had compassion* on her and said to her, 'Do not weep.' And he came and touched the bier, and the bearers stood still. And he said, 'Young man, I say to you, arise.' And the dead man sat up, and began to speak.

—towards the socially unacceptable:

Now the tax collectors and sinners were all drawing near to hear him. And the Pharisees and the scribes murmured, saying, 'This man receives sinners and eats with them.'

Anger

▷ Jesus had many angry words to say to the religious leaders who, by their teaching and behaviour, were distorting or denying the truth for which Jesus had such deeply-felt concern:

Well did Isaiah prophesy of you hypocrites . . . You leave the commandment of God, and hold fast the tradition of men . . . You have a fine way of rejecting the commandment of God, in order to keep your tradition!

Woe to you, scribes and Pharisees, hypocrites! because you shut the kingdom of heaven against men; for you neither enter yourselves, nor allow those who would enter to go in . . .

Woe to you, blind guides . . . you blind fools!

Woe to you, scribes and Pharisees, hypocrites! for you cleanse the outside of the cup and of the plate, but inside they are full of extortion and rapacity . . . You . . outwardly appear righteous to men, but within you are full of hypocrisy and iniquity.

He entered the temple and began to drive out those who sold and those who bought in the temple, and he overturned the tables of the money-changers and the seats of those who sold pigeons; and he would not allow any one to carry anything through the temple. And he taught, and said to them, 'Is it not written, "My house shall be called a house of prayer for all the nations"? But you have made it a den of robbers.'

▷ The reaction of Jesus to the death of his friend, Lazarus, reveals both compassion and anger in the face of death:

When Jesus saw her weeping, and the Jews who came with her also weeping, he was deeply moved in spirit and troubled; and he said, 'Where have you laid him?' They said to him, 'Lord, come and see.' Jesus wept. So the Jews said, 'See how he loved him!'

Humility

▷ Jesus' humility before God:

I can do nothing on my own authority . . . I seek not my own will but the will of him who sent me.

I have come down from heaven, not to do my own will, but the will of him who sent me.

▷ His humility before men. Luke describes this incident at the Last Supper:

A dispute also arose among them, which of them was to be regarded as the greatest. And he said to them, 'The kings of the Gentiles exercise lordship over them; and those in authority over them are called benefactors. But not so with you; rather let the greatest among them become as the youngest, and the leader as one who serves. For which is the greater, one who sits at table, or one who serves? Is it not the one who sits at table? But I am among you as one who serves.

After the supper, he demonstrated in action something of what he meant by the outlook of the servant:

Jesus, knowing that the Father had given all things into his hands, and that he had come from God and was going to God, rose from supper, laid aside his garments, and girded himself with a towel. Then he poured water into a basin, and began to wash the disciples' feet, and to wipe them with the towel with which he was girded . . .

When he had washed their feet, and taken his garments and resumed his place, he said to them, 'Do you know what I have done to you? You call me Teacher and Lord; and you are right, for so I am. If I then, your Lord and Teacher, have washed your feet, you also ought to wash one another's feet. For I have given you an example, that you also should do as I have done to you.'

Goodness

▷ People acknowledged the positive goodness of what Jesus was doing:

And they were astonished beyond measure, saying, 'He has done all things well; he even makes the deaf hear and the dumb speak.'

▷ He himself claimed to be without sin:

Which of you convicts me of sin?

▷ His disciples claimed that he was sinless:

He committed no sin; no guile was found on his lips. When he was reviled, he did not revile in return; when he suffered, he did not threaten; but he trusted to him who judges justly.

If we say we have no sin, we deceive ourselves . . . He appeared to take away sins, and in him there is no sin.

HIS CLAIMS ABOUT HIMSELF

His claim to be the Son

He spoke of himself as 'the Son' and of God as 'the Father' or 'my Father'.

Of that day or that hour (the day of judgement) no one knows, not even the angels in heaven, nor *the Son*, but only *the Father*.

All things have been delivered to me by *my Father;* and no one knows *the Son* except *the Father*, and no one knows *the Father* except *the Son* and any one to whom *the Son* chooses to reveal him.

Whoever does the will of *my Father* in heaven is my brother.

The Son of man is to come with his angels in the glory of *his Father*.

I and *the Father* are one.

The Father judges no one, but has given all judgement to *the Son*, that all may honour

The religious leaders of Jesus' day felt the full force of his anger when he called them 'whited sepulchres.' Like whitewashed tombs they were clean-looking outside, but rotten within.

the Son, even as they honour *the Father*. He who does not honour *the Son* does not honour *the Father* who sent him.

No one comes to *the Father*, but by me. If you had known me, you would have known *my Father* also.

His claim to be the fulfilment of the Old Testament

The time is fulfilled (i.e. the time spoken about by the prophets), and the kingdom of God is at hand.

The Son of man also came . . . to serve, and to give his life as a ransom for many.
   (These are allusions to the Son of man described in Daniel 7 and the Suffering Servant in Isaiah 42-53.)

This is my blood of the covenant, which is poured out for many.
   (An allusion to the blood of the Old Testament sacrifices, the covenant which God made with the nation at Sinai, and the 'new covenant' spoken of by Ezekiel and Jeremiah.)

The high priest asked him, 'Are you the Christ, the Son of the Blessed?' And Jesus said, 'I am; and you will see the Son of man sitting at the right hand of Power, and coming with the clouds of heaven.'
   (Another reference to the Son of man in Daniel.)

He opened the book and found the place where it was written, 'The Spirit of the Lord is upon me . . .' And he began to say to them, 'Today this scripture has been fulfilled in your hearing.'
   (He was reading from a passage in Isaiah.)

Everything written about me in the law of Moses and the prophets and the psalms must be fulfilled . . . Thus it is written, that the Christ should suffer and on the third day rise from the dead.

The scriptures . . . bear witness to me.

If you believed Moses, you would believe me, for he wrote of me.

His indirect claims

Jesus claimed to be able to do things which, according to Jewish belief, only God could do.

▷ He forgave sins:

Jesus . . . said to the paralytic, 'My son, your sins are forgiven.' Now some of the scribes were sitting there, questioning in their hearts, 'Why does this man speak thus? It is blasphemy! Who can forgive sins but God alone?' And . . . Jesus . . . said . . . '. . . the Son of man has authority on earth to forgive sins.'

▷ He claimed to be able to give eternal life:

As the Father raises the dead and gives them life, so also the Son gives life to whom he will.

I am the resurrection and the life; he who believes in me, though he die, yet shall he live.

▷ He claimed to teach the truth with authority:

You have heard that it was said to the men of old, 'You shall not kill . . . .' But I say to you . . .

Heaven and earth will pass away, but my words will not pass away.

For this I have come into the world, to bear witness to the truth. Every one who is of the truth hears my voice.

▷ He said he would one day judge the world:

When the Son of man comes in his glory, and

all the angels with him, then he will sit on his glorious throne. Before him will be gathered all the nations, and he will separate them one from another as a shepherd separates the sheep from the goats.

The Father judges no one, but has given all judgement to the Son, that all may honour the Son, even as they honour the Father.

▷ He claimed to be able to satisfy the deepest needs of men, and he invited them to follow him and give him their allegiance:

Come to me, all who labour and are heavy laden, and I will give you rest. Take my yoke upon you, and learn from me; for I am gentle and lowly in heart, and you will find rest for your souls.

If any one comes to me and does not hate his own father and mother . . . and even his own life, he cannot be my disciple.

If any one thirst, let him come to me and drink.

This is the work of God, that you believe in him whom he has sent.

Believe in God, believe also in me.

HIS MIRACLES

Three different kinds of miracle are recorded.

▷ Nature miracles: e.g. stilling the storm (Mark 4: 35-41); feeding the 5,000 with five loaves and two fishes (Mark 6: 30–44); walking on the water (Mark 6: 45–52); changing the water into wine (John 2: 1–11).

▷ Healing miracles: e.g. healing of fever, leprosy, blindness, demon possession, etc.

▷ Raising from death: e.g. the son of the woman of Nain (Luke 7: 11–17); Lazarus of Bethany (John 11: 1–53).

The Gospels record Jesus' motives in performing the miracles.

▷ Compassion:

As they went out of Jericho, a great crowd followed him. And behold, two blind men sitting

---

The scrolls of the Torah, the Old Testament law, being carried into a newly consecrated synagogue. Jesus claimed to be the fulfilment of the law.

by the roadside, when they heard that Jesus was passing by, cried out, 'Have mercy on us, Son of David!' . . . Jesus stopped and called them, saying, 'What do you want me to do for you?' They said to him, 'Lord, let our eyes be opened.' And Jesus *in pity* touched their eyes, and immediately they received their sight and followed him.

In those days, when again a great crowd had gathered, and they had nothing to eat, he called his disciples to him, and said to them, '*I have compassion* on the crowd, because they have been with me now three days, and have nothing to eat . . .'

▷ The glory of God. Many of the miracles led people to give glory to God:

. . . so that the throng wondered, when they saw the dumb speaking, the maimed whole, the lame walking, and the blind seeing; and they glorified the God of Israel.

▷ Evidence to support his claims:

And immediately Jesus, perceiving in his spirit that they thus questioned within themselves, said to them, 'Why do you question thus in your hearts? Which is easier, to say to the paralytic "Your sins are forgiven," or to say, "Rise, take up your pallet and walk"? But *that you may know that the Son of man has authority* on earth to forgive sins'—he said to the paralytic—'I say to you, rise, take up your pallet and go home.' And he rose, and immediately took up the pallet and went out before them all . . .

When John heard in prison about the deeds of the Christ, he sent word by his disciples and said to him, 'Are you he who is to come, or shall we look for another?' And Jesus answered them, 'Go and tell John what you hear and see: the blind receive their sight and the lame walk, lepers are cleansed and the deaf hear, and the dead are raised up, and the poor have good news preached to them.

If I am not doing the works of my Father, then do not believe me; but if I do them, even though you do not believe me, believe the works, *that you may know and understand* that the Father is in me and I am in the Father.

There were times, however, when people pressed him to work miracles not out of a genuine desire to be convinced, but out of a defiant scepticism. And on these occasions, Jesus refused to work miracles to order:

The Pharisees came and began to argue with

him, seeking from him a sign from heaven, to test him. And he sighed deeply in his spirit, and said, 'Why does this generation seek a sign? Truly, I say to you, no sign shall be given to this generation.' And he left them.

Matthew's version of this saying (Matthew 12: 39–40) adds an exception which points forward to the resurrection as the one and only sign which he would give these proud Pharisees.

PEOPLE'S REACTIONS

How did people react to the man Jesus? These are some of the earliest reactions to Jesus, as recorded by Mark:

. . . they were astonished at his teaching, for he taught them as one who had authority . . . (1:22)

. . . they were all amazed and glorified God, saying, 'We never saw anything like this!' (2:12)

. . . they said, 'He is beside himself.' (3:21)

. . . they were filled with awe, and said to one another, 'Who then is this, that even wind and sea obey him?' (4:41)

. . . they were afraid . . . and they began to beg Jesus to depart from their neighbourhood. (5:15, 17)

. . . many who heard him were astonished, saying, 'Where did this man get all this? What is the wisdom given to him? What mighty works are wrought by his hands! Is not this the carpenter, the son of Mary and brother of James and Joses and Judas and Simon, and are not his sisters here with us?' (6:2–3)

they were astonished beyond measure, saying, 'He has done all things well; he even makes the deaf hear and the dumb speak.' (7:37)

In our study of the evidence about Jesus, we have to get beyond these initial reactions and make up our minds about the deeper issue: what was the relationship of this man Jesus to God? Our answer will depend not only on how we interpret the evidence of the Gospels, but also on our assumptions about the meaning of the word 'God'.

Anyone who believes in the existence of a personal God will probably find little difficulty in accepting the following assumptions about the meaning of the word 'God':

☐ that he is a being who exists;

□ that he is personal and infinite;

□ that he is the Creator and Sustainer of the universe;

□ that he is loving and holy;

□ that he is one (the precise nature of this oneness does not need to be defined at this stage; it can be left an open question for the time being).

If we cannot accept these assumptions, or if we cannot even accept them for the time

Leprosy sufferers waiting patiently for attention at a village clinic in India. Jesus healed lepers – and his followers have led the fight against the disease, which can now be cured.

being as a working hypothesis, then we should consider first the other possible answers to the question about God. There is little point in discussing Jesus' relationship with 'God' if we do not have at least some measure of agreement about the meaning of the word 'God' (see further BOOK TWO, pp. 9ff.).

What was Jesus' relationship to God?

"He was a prophet sent by God" PAGE 23

"He was a created being from heaven" PAGE 20

"He was a man and nothing more" PAGE 30

"He was both man and God; he was the Son of God" PAGE 17

"He was only a man—but also a revelation of 'God'" PAGE 33

ANSWER 1: BIBLICAL CHRISTIANITY

"He was both man and God; he was the Son of God"

He was fully human and fully divine. He was a real human being; but at the same time he was God the Son, the second person of the Trinity, who had existed with the Father and the Spirit from eternity.

The first disciples could not have expressed their beliefs about Jesus in these terms *during* his lifetime. But they spoke of him as God's Messiah, i.e. God's Anointed Agent for working out his purposes in the world. And they used words and titles for him which a Jew would reserve exclusively for the one true God:

Peter said: 'You are the Christ' (Mark 8: 29)

Thomas said: 'My Lord and my God!' (John 20: 28)

The disciples said: 'We have believed and have come to know, that you are the Holy One of God.' (John 6: 69)

'We believe that you came from God.' (John 16: 30)

The words which they used *after* his lifetime do not go beyond these claims. They identify him fully *both* with man *and* with God:

Since therefore the children share in flesh and blood, he himself likewise partook of the same nature, that through death he might destroy him who has the power of death.

We have not a high priest who is unable to sympathize with our weaknesses, but one who in every respect has been tempted as we are, yet without sinning.

. . . the Lord of glory . . .

. . . the . . . man . . . from heaven . . .

. . . Christ Jesus, who, though he was in the form of God, did not count equality with God a thing to be grasped, but emptied himself, taking the form of a servant, being born in the likeness of men. And being found in human form he humbled himself and became obedient unto death, even death on a cross. Therefore God has highly exalted him and bestowed on him the name which is above every name, that at the name of Jesus every knee should bow, in heaven and on earth and under the earth, and every tongue confess that Jesus Christ is Lord, to the glory of God the Father.

HOW DOES THIS ANSWER MAKE SENSE OF THE EVIDENCE?

Christ's birth

The narratives make perfect sense if the baby was human and divine at the same time. If his conception had been totally natural, he could not in any sense have been anything other than, or more than, a human being.

His character

Jesus' compassion can be seen as something more than ordinary human compassion; it becomes a demonstration in practice of the love of God for man.

His anger is not the purely human feeling

of rage, which results from frustration, or wounded pride, or selfish indignation; it becomes an expression of the hatred of the holy God towards anything which denies him, or distorts the truth, or degrades man.

His humility is the humility of the Son who has humbled himself before the Father to become man and to live as a man; and because he is utterly humble before the Father and is empty of self, he can be humble before men.

His goodness is not an inevitable or automatic perfection. As a real man he experienced all kinds of temptations, but he relied on the power of the Holy Spirit and was obedient to the word of the Father.

His claims

Jesus' claims about himself are not the ravings of a megalomaniac or the subtle deceptions of a man who wants to gain power; they simply express the closest possible personal relationship between Jesus and the Father.

His miracles

Jesus' miracles make sense as demonstrations of the love and compassion of God which would lead men to give all the credit and the glory to God. And they also provide further evidence to substantiate his claims to have come from God and to be doing the work of God.

SOME IMPLICATIONS OF THIS ANSWER

▷ If Jesus is both God and man, *he can be a perfect revelation of God to men.*

He can reveal God adequately because he himself is fully divine:

No one has ever seen God; *the only Son, who is in the bosom of the Father*, he has made him known.

This revelation is in a form that can be grasped fully by men; they can perceive it through hearing, through sight and through touch:

That which was from the beginning, which we have *heard*, which we have *seen* with our eyes, which we have *looked upon* and *touched with our hands*, concerning the word of life—the life was made manifest, and we *saw* it, and testify to it, and proclaim to you the eternal life which was with the Father and was made manifest to us—that which we have *seen* and *heard* we proclaim also to you, so that you may have fellowship with us . . .

▷ If Jesus is both God and man, *he is in a position to deal with the moral problem of man.* As a man, he lived a life of complete obedience to the Father, and he was obedient right to the point of death.

His life of obedience can therefore be the reversal of the disobedience of Adam. His complete obedience has the effect of undoing the consequences of the sin of Adam:

. . . sin came into the world through one man and death through sin, and so death spread

to all men because all men sinned . . . But the free gift is not like the trespass. For if many died through one man's trespass, much more have the grace of God and the free gift in the grace of *that one man Jesus Christ* abounded for many. . . . If, because of one man's trespass, death reigned through that one man, much more will those who receive the abundance of grace and the free gift of righteousness reign in life through *the one man Jesus Christ*. Then as one man's trespass led to condemnation for all men, so *one man's act of righteousness* leads to acquittal and life for all men. For as by one man's disobedience many were made sinners, so by *one man's obedience* many will be made righteous.

Because he himself is fully divine, what *he* does, *God* does in him:

All is from God, who through Christ reconciled the world to himself . . . *God was in Christ* reconciling the world to himself, not counting their trespasses against them . . .

Because he is fully human, he can identify himself with men and the guilt of their sin:

There is one God, and there is one mediator between God and men, *the man Christ Jesus*, who gave himself as a ransom for all . . .

▷ The fact that Jesus is both divine and human *can mean something in the present experience of the Christian.* Jesus is still fully human in heaven. He did not discard his humanity as if it were a garment which he could take off. There is therefore no need for any further mediator (such as Mary or the saints). There can be no one in heaven who is 'more human' and tender and compassionate than Jesus himself.

He had to be made like his brethren in every respect, so that he might become a merciful and faithful high priest in the service of God . . . For because he himself has suffered and been tempted, he is able to help those who are tempted.

We have not a high priest who is unable to sympathize with our weaknesses, but one who in every respect has been tempted as we are, yet without sinning. Let us then with confidence draw near to the throne of grace, that we may receive mercy and find grace to help in time of need.

▷ When the Christian puts his faith in Jesus Christ as the one who is fully God and fully man, *he is united with him in the closest possible union*. It is not a union in which the believer is absorbed into God, but a union in which he retains his identity and even experiences the love that there is between the Father and the Son. This was the kind of union for which Jesus prayed before his arrest. It is possible because Jesus is perfectly one *both* with God *and* with man.

I do not pray for these only, but also for those who are to believe in me through their word, that they may all be one; even as thou, Father, art in me, and I in thee, that they also may be in us, so that the world may believe that thou hast sent me. The glory which thou hast given me I have given to them, that they may be one even as we are one, I in them and thou in me, that they may become perfectly one, so that the world may know that thou hast sent me and hast loved them even as thou hast loved me. Father, I desire that they also, whom thou hast given me, may be with me where I am, to behold my glory which thou hast given me in thy love for me before the foundation of the world. O righteous Father, the world has not known thee, but I have known thee; and these know that thou hast sent me. I have made known to them thy name, and I will make it known, that the love with which thou hast loved me may be in them and I in them.

If you give this answer, you should go on to consider the meaning of the death of Jesus, pp. 49 ff.

A model of the high priest in his robes. Aaron, the first high priest, was the appointed intermediary between a holy God and a sinful people.

ANSWER 2

"He was a created being from heaven"

This is to say, Jesus was more than an ordinary man; but he was not God in any sense. He was the 'Son of God' in the sense that he was a supernatural being from heaven—but a created being.

This answer has taken several different forms throughout the course of history. It was, for example, the teaching of *Arius of Alexandria* in the fourth century.

In our own day, *Jehovah's Witnesses* teach that Jesus was a created spirit from heaven:

That Jesus might save his people from their sin, it was necessary that the Son of God be born as a human creature and grow to become 'the man Christ Jesus' . . . None of Adam's offspring being sinless or having the right life to offer as a redemptive price, it was necessary for the Son of God to lay aside his spirit existence and become the needed perfect man, no more, no less. Thus Jesus could die, not as a spirit creature, but as a perfect human creature, for humankind needing redemption. For these and other reasons Jesus was not a 'God-man', for that would be more than the required price of redemption. Had he been immortal God or an immortal soul he could not have given his life. According to the Scriptural facts, he was mortal on earth . . .
The primary purpose of the Son of God in coming to earth was to meet and decisively answer Satan's false charge that God cannot

put on earth a creature who will keep his integrity and abide faithful till death under the test of persecution from the Devil and his demons . . .

They believe that Jesus was appointed to be the Son of God at the time of his baptism:

John heard God's voice announcing Jesus as His Son. This proves that God there begot Jesus by his Spirit or active force, by virtue of which Jesus now became the spiritual Son of God, possessing the right to spirit life in heaven. God so begot him, because Jesus' right to human life was henceforth to be dedicated to redeeming humankind. . . .
God's prophecy, at Psalm 2:7, was directed to Jesus: 'Thou art my Son; this day I have begotten thee.' When Jehovah begot the baptized Jesus and made him the spiritual Son of God with right to life in the heavenly spirit realm, Jesus became a 'new creature'.

He thus became immortal after his death on the cross:

In due time, after proving his faithfulness to death and providing redemption from sin, the Son was rewarded with immortality.

POINTS TO CONSIDER ABOUT THIS ANSWER

This answer is based on a very selective reading of the New Testament. It makes

some sense of verses which speak of Jesus' dependence on the Father and his humility before the Father. But it ignores all the other evidence which points to a much closer relationship with the Father.

The verses which are claimed to support this interpretation can hardly bear the weight that is put on them; as the three following examples show.

▷ The Father is greater than I.

These words must be understood in the light of all the other sayings of Jesus in John's Gospel, for example:

I and the Father are one.

He who has seen me has seen the Father; how can you say, 'Show us the Father'? Do you not believe that I am in the Father and the Father in me?

These words therefore point to the way in which the eternal Son humbled himself before the Father, for the work of revelation and salvation. Paul writes about the humbling and self-emptying of the Son in this way:

. . . Christ Jesus . . . though he was in the form of God, did not count equality with God a thing to be grasped, but emptied himself, taking the form of a servant, being born in the likeness of men . . .

▷ Why do you call me good? No one is good but God alone.

Jesus gave this answer in reply to the person who asked him:

Good Teacher, what shall I do to inherit eternal life?

A Jehovah's Witness is baptized at a mass baptism at a local swimming-pool. Jehovah's Witnesses believe that Jesus became the 'Son of God' at his baptism.

Jesus was probably testing the man to see whether his words were a casual compliment, or whether he had realized who Jesus was. Or he could be saying, 'If you think I am no more than an ordinary human teacher, why do you call me good?' Whatever the exact interpretation of these words, Jesus goes on to make a very big claim for himself. He does not argue with the man when he claims that he has kept all the commandments. Instead he takes it upon himself to tell the man where he is still falling short, and tells him to become a disciple:

One thing you still lack. Sell all that you have and distribute to the poor, and you will have treasure in heaven; and come, follow me.

▷ He is the image of the invisible God, the first-born of all creation . . .

The remaining verses of this passage show that the writer did *not* believe that Jesus was a created being. On the contrary, *everything* both in heaven and on earth was created through him:

He is the image of the invisible God, the first-born of all creation; for in him all things were created, in heaven and on earth, visible and invisible, whether thrones or dominions or principalities or authorities—all things were created through him and for him. He is before all things, and in him all things hold together. . . .

C. F. D. Moule explains the two possible interpretations of the word 'first-born':

(i) Translate the 'first–' as a *time-metaphor* . . . Translated thus, it may allude to Christ's priority to the created world: he was born (or, as more considered theology would say, begotten, not born) before any created thing . . .
(ii) Take 'firstborn' not as a temporal term so much as in the sense of *supreme*— 'the one who is supreme over all creation' . . . If one must choose, there is, perhaps, a little more to be said in favour of (ii) . . . But possibly (i) and (ii) are to be combined: 'prior to and supreme over'.

Other passages of the New Testament expressly reject this kind of interpretation. The writer of the letter to the Hebrews, for example, was aware of beliefs which made Jesus an exalted being, but a being created by God. He emphasizes the gulf which separates Jesus, the Son, from all the created angels in heaven:

In many and various ways God spoke of old to our fathers by the prophets; but in these last days he has spoken to us by a Son, whom he appointed heir of all things, through whom also he created the world. He reflects the glory of God and bears the very stamp of his nature, upholding the universe by his word of power. When he had made purification for sin, he sat down at the right hand of the Majesty on high, having become as much superior to angels as the name he has obtained is more excellent than theirs.

If you give this kind of answer, you must think of Jesus as a mediator who is less than God. Being less than God, he cannot do anything more than reveal messages from God, and he cannot deal with the guilt of man before the holy God. He can act to some extent on behalf of men if he is fully man, but he cannot take it upon himself to forgive sin. Since it is God himself who has been wronged, and God himself whose laws have been broken, *only God* can forgive the wrong and the disobedience. If Jesus were less than God, he could not act on behalf of God in dealing with the moral problem of man.

This answer is usually based not only on a selective reading of the New Testament, but also on certain assumptions about God and man.

It is assumed that the gulf between God and man is so great that Godhead and humanity cannot possibly be combined in a single personality.

It is also assumed that God is one in the strictly literal sense, so that there cannot possibly be any kind of diversity within the unity. This is the assumption behind the teaching of Jehovah's Witnesses: Jehovah is, by definition, 'one' in the most literal sense:

If Jesus had been Almighty God Jehovah he could not save his people from their sin, by his blood, because Jehovah God is immortal, 'from everlasting to everlasting'. . . . Almighty God cannot die, but Jesus could die and did die, as testified by the Scriptures; hence he could not be God his Father, but was God's mortal Son.

See further, BOOK TWO, Question Two, 'Who or what is God?' and Question Three, 'What is man?'

ANSWER 3

"He was a prophet sent by God"

Many Jews recognize that Jesus was a godly man who brought a real message from God to his fellow men. Islam goes further and affirms that Jesus was one of the great prophets sent by God.

In the first few centuries after the death of Jesus, although most Jews did not recognize Jesus as Messiah, they were not totally unsympathetic to him. Later, however, more critical attitudes were expressed.

Herbert Danby, writing about the Jewish traditions recorded in the *Talmud:*

Here is the sum-total of all that the Talmud is *alleged* (sometimes rightly, but more often wrongly) to say of Christianity's Founder:
    A certain Yeshu, called the Notsri, or the Son of Stada, or the Son of Pantera, was born out of wedlock. His mother was called Miriam. She was a woman's hairdresser (the word here is *M'gadd'la*, a pun on the name Mary Magdalen). Her husband was Pappus, the son of Yehudah, and her paramour a Roman soldier, Pantera. She is said to have been the descendant of princes and rulers. This Yeshu had been to Egypt, whence he brought back the knowledge of many tricks and sorcery. He was just a sorcerer, and so deceived and led astray the people of Israel; he sinned and caused the multitude to sin. He made a mock of the words of the learned men and was excommunicated. He was tainted with heresy. He called himself God and said that he would go up to heaven. He was tried before the Court at Lud on a charge of being a deceiver and teacher of apostasy. Evidence was produced against him by concealing witnesses to hear his statements, and a lamp was so placed that his face could be seen, but so that he could not see the witnesses. He was executed in Lud on the Eve of Passover, which fell on the eve of a Sabbath. During

forty days a herald proclaimed that Yeshu was to be stoned, and evidence was invited in his favour, but none was forthcoming. He was stoned and hanged. Under the name of Balaam he was put to death by 'Pinhas the Robber' (supposed to refer to Pontius Pilate). At the time he was thirty-three years old. He was punished in Gehenna by means of boiling scum. He was 'near to the kingdom' (whatever that may mean). He had five disciples: Mattai, Naqai, Netser, Buni and Today. Under the name of Balaam he was excluded from the world to come.

The following articles from the *Jewish Encyclopedia* sum up the attitude of many Jews in the twentieth century to Jesus.

His birth:

The supernatural in the life of Jesus according to the Gospels is restricted to the smallest dimensions, consisting mainly of incidents and characteristics intended to support these prophecies (from the Old Testament) and the dogmatic positions of Christianity. This applies especially to the story of the virgin-birth, a legend which is common to almost all folk-heroes as indicating their superiority to the rest of their people.

His claims:

The Prophets spoke with confidence in the truth of their message, but expressly on the ground that they were declaring the word of the Lord. Jesus adopted equal confidence, but he emphasised his own authority apart from any vicarious

Orthodox Jewish worship still continues in this Jerusalem synagogue.

or deputed authority from on high. Yet in doing so he did not—at any rate publicly—ever lay claim to any authority as attaching to his position as Messiah.

The most striking characteristic of the utterances of Jesus, regarded as a personality, were the tone of authority adopted by him and the claim that spiritual peace and salvation were to be found in the mere acceptance of his leadership. Passages like Matt. 11:29, 8:35, 25:40 indicate an assumption of power which is certainly unique in Jewish history, and indeed account for much of modern Jewish antipathy to Jesus, so far as it exists. On the other hand, there is little in any of these utterances to show that they were meant by the speaker to apply to anything more than personal relations with him; and it might well be that in his experience he found that spiritual relief was often afforded by simple human trust in his good-will and power of direction.

This . . . raises the question whether Jesus regarded himself as in any sense a Messiah or spiritual ruler; and there is singularly little evidence in the synoptic Gospels to carry out this claim. These assert only that the claim was made to some of the disciples, and then under a distinct pledge of secrecy. In the public utterances of Jesus there is absolutely no trace of the claim (except possibly in the use of the expression 'Son of man'). Yet it would almost appear that in one sense of the word Jesus regarded himself as fulfilling some of the prophesies which were taken among contemporary Jews as applying to the Messiah. In other words, Jesus regarded himself as typically human, and claimed authority and regard in that respect.

His miracles:

It is difficult to estimate what amount of truth exists in the accounts of these cures, recorded about forty years after their occurrence; but doubtless the mental excitement due to the influence of Jesus was often efficacious in at least partial or temporary cures of mental illness. This would tend to confirm the impression, both among those who witnessed the cures and among his disciples, of his possession of supernatural powers. He himself occasionally deprecated the exaggeration to which such cures naturally led.

Other Jews have expressed an attitude which is considerably more sympathetic.

Claude Montefiore:

The most important Jew who ever lived, one who exercised a greater influence upon mankind and civilization than any other person, whether within the Jewish race or without it . . . A Jew whose life and character have been regarded by almost all the best and wisest people who have heard or read of his actions and his words, as the greatest religious exemplar of every age.

God's nearness was felt by Jesus directly with a vivid intensity unsurpassed by any man.

Sholem Asch:

What was quite new in the teaching of Jesus was that for the first time there appeared in Israel a teacher who, while in agreement with the law of Moses, did not derive his authority from that law . . . He appealed to an authority which had been entrusted to his keeping . . . The Jews were bound to the authority which had been given to Moses on Sinai, and which they had recognized with their promise of obedience. They could not pass to the new authority without the sign which should proclaim that the old had been cancelled and the new one validated . . . The first coming of the Messiah was not for us but for the Gentiles.

It is only right to admit that it was the shameful way in which Christians began to treat the Jews that made Jews take a more hostile attitude to Jesus. It is Christians who are largely responsible for preventing Jews from getting a fair and accurate picture of Jesus.

Herbert Danby:

We are forced to the conclusion that so long as Pharisaic Judaism (which, we must remember, was the only form of Judaism which survived the destruction of Jerusalem)—so long as it records personal or almost personal reminiscence of our Lord, the surviving record is not viciously hostile (as later became the case); but the farther the Jews were removed from the time of our Lord's earthly life, and the more dependent they became for knowledge of Jesus upon later generations of *Christians*, then so much worse became the Jewish characterization of Jesus.

Writing about the Jewish Talmud:

In the main the Jews had already begun the process which has characterized a great part of Judaism even to the present day—the process of slamming the door, and locking, barring and bolting his mind against the whole subject of Christianity.

Sholem Asch, novelist and dramatist, born in Poland in 1880.

POINTS TO CONSIDER ABOUT THIS ANSWER

Some of these observations (particularly in the *Jewish Encyclopedia*) are hardly consistent with the Gospels as we have them.

How could orthodox Palestinian Jews introduce elements from pagan legends to describe the birth of Jesus, knowing that by doing so they denied the most fundamental article of their faith, the one-ness of God?

Is it really true to say that Jesus never claimed any authority deputed by the Father? What of his claims to be 'the Son'?

Granted that he did not claim openly to be *the Messiah;* did he not make many other direct and indirect claims in which he identified himself with *God himself?*

How could a Jew invite fellow Jews to find comfort in personal relations with him by using language which associated him so closely with God, and which ignored the difference between the creature and the Creator?

This answer is usually based on the assumption that the Gospels cannot be an objective or reliable account of what Jesus said and did.

Because the Gospels, while containing valuable material, are all written in a polemical spirit and for the purpose of substantiating the claim of the Messianic spirit and superhuman character of Jesus, it is difficult to present an impartial story of his life.

If there can be no agreement about the Gospel evidence, the discussion must turn on assumptions about God and man. If, for example, you approach the Gospels with your mind already made up that God is one in the strictly literal sense, and if no amount of evidence will persuade you to revise your understanding of what this one-ness means, then you must consider some of the problems involved in this concept of the one-ness of God. (See BOOK TWO, Question Three, 'Who or what is God?', pp. 9 ff.)

ISLAM

The Qur'an has its own accounts of the different aspects of the life of Jesus, who is known as 'Esa, son of Mary'.

His birth:

'I am the messenger of your Lord,' he (Gabriel) replied, 'and have come to give you a holy son.'
'How shall I bear a child,' she answered, 'when I am a virgin, untouched by man?'
'Such is the will of your Lord,' he replied. 'This is no difficult thing for Him. "He shall be a sign to mankind," says the Lord, "and a blessing from Ourself. That is Our decree." ' Thereupon she conceived . . .

And remember the angel's words to Mary. He said: 'Allah has chosen you. He has made you pure and exalted you above all women . . .'

His character:

There are many references to Jesus, but it is not possible to build up any picture of his character. Islam, however, seems to share the belief that Jesus was sinless. Although it speaks of the sins of all the other great prophets, Adam, Noah, Abraham, Moses, and Mohammed, it nowhere attributes any sin to Jesus. This conclusion is expressed in one of the *Traditions:*

Every child born of Adam is touched by Satan the day his mother is delivered of him with the exception of Mary and her son.

His claims:

None of Jesus' claims for himself are quoted. But the Qur'an gives the following titles to Jesus:

'the Messiah'
'the Word of God'

'the Sure Saying'
'a spirit sent from God'
'the Messenger of God', or 'the Apostle of God'
'the Servant of God'
'the Prophet of God'

The Messiah, Jesus the son of Mary, was no more than Allah's apostle and His Word which he cast to Mary: a spirit from Him.

To these titles we can add two further claims made about Jesus in the *Traditions:*

He will be an Intercessor in heaven. The Qur'an says of Jesus 'God took him to himself', implying that Jesus is now alive in heaven. Another verse describes Jesus as 'worthy of regard in this world and in that to come'.

Baidhawi, an authoritative commentator, interprets these words in this way:

In this world as Prophet, in the next as an Intercessor.

He will be a judge.

There is no doubt that the Son of Mary, on whom be blessing and peace, shall descend in the midst of you as a righteous judge.

His miracles:

▷ Jesus, while still a baby, defends his mother against those who think she has been immoral and had a child out of wedlock:

Then she took her child to her people, who said to her: 'This is indeed a strange thing! Sister of Aaron, your father was never a wicked man, nor was your mother a harlot.'
She made a sign to them, pointing to the child. But they replied: 'How can we speak with a new-born infant?'
Whereupon he spoke and said: 'I am the servant of Allah. He has given me the Gospel and ordained me a prophet. His blessing is upon me wherever I go, and He has commanded me to be steadfast in prayer and to give alms to the poor as long as I shall live . . .'

▷ This miracle of the table spread with food sent from heaven contains echoes of the miracle of the feeding of the 5,000 as recorded in the Gospels:

'Jesus, son of Mary,' said the disciples, 'can Allah send down to us from heaven a table spread with food?'
He replied: 'Have fear of Allah, if you are true believers.'
'We wish to eat of it,' they said, 'so that we may reassure our hearts and know that what you said to us is true, and that we may be witnesses of it.'
'Lord,' said Jesus, the son of Mary, 'send to us from heaven a table spread with food, that it may mark a feast for us and our sustenance; You are the best Giver.'
Allah replied: 'I am sending one to you. But whoever of you disbelieves hereafter shall be punished as no man has ever been punished.'

▷ This summary of his miracles refers to the story, found also in one of the apocryphal gospels, of Jesus making clay birds come to life:

Allah will say: 'Jesus, son of Mary, remember the favour I have bestowed on you and on your mother: how I strengthened you with the Holy Spirit, so that you preached to men in your cradle and in the prime of manhood; how I instructed you in the Scriptures and in wisdom, in the Torah and in the Gospel; how by My leave you fashioned from clay the likeness of a bird and breathed into it so that, by My leave, it became a living bird; how, by My leave, you healed the blind man and the leper, and by My leave restored the dead to life; how I protected you from the Israelites when you brought them veritable signs: when the unbelievers among them said: "This is nothing but plain magic"; how when I enjoined the disciples to believe in Me and in my Apostle they replied: "We believe; bear witness that we submit to You utterly." '

POINTS TO CONSIDER ABOUT THIS ANSWER

From the above passages it is obvious that the Qur'an puts Jesus in a unique position. This is a position not shared by any of the other prophets, not even by Mohammed who

A Moslem in Java begins an hour of meditation and readings from the Qur'an.

is said to be the last and greatest of the prophets:

▷ The birth of Jesus was a miraculous virgin birth; the words of annunciation addressed to Mary are not paralleled by any similar words addressed to Amina, the mother of Mohammed.

▷ No sin of any kind is attributed to Jesus; but all the other five great prophets need to seek forgiveness from God.

▷ Of the titles given to Jesus, some are exactly the same as the titles given to Mohammed: 'the Messenger of God', 'the Servant of God', 'the Prophet of God'. But the other titles given to Jesus are given to no other prophet: 'the Messiah', 'the Word of God', 'the Sure Saying', 'a spirit sent from God'. Whereas Jesus can be thought of as an intercessor, Mohammed explicitly disclaims the right to intercede for sinners before God.

And whereas Jesus is said to have been raised to heaven, Mohammed is dead and has not yet been raised to be with God in heaven.

▷ Later traditions attributed miracles to Mohammed. But according to the Qur'an, he consistently disclaimed power to work miracles. When he was challenged to produce his credentials and to prove that he was a prophet sent from God, he pointed to the Qur'an as being sufficient miracle in itself.

But why is Jesus so unique if Mohammed is the greatest prophet and the final messenger from God?

And what of the many questions left unanswered in the Qur'an? Why is Jesus called 'the Messiah'? Why his miraculous birth? What precisely was his Message, his Ingil? The Jesus of the Qur'an remains something of an enigma.

Henri Michaud in his study of Jesus according to the Qur'an:

After having tried to understand what the

Qur'an says about Jesus, we shall ask our brothers of Islam with very great anxiety: 'Is this indeed what you believe about Jesus?' If there is a reply without ambiguity, then an irenical dialogue can be begun.

If you accept the Qur'an as a reliable source of evidence about Jesus, but are not satisfied with the incompleteness of this picture, are you willing to *supplement* it with the fuller picture of Jesus in the Gospels? And are you willing to consider how the Gospels answer these questions? (See pp. 9ff.)

The Qur'an's rejection of the Christian understanding of Jesus is based to some extent on a misunderstanding.
   It may be that the Trinity which Mohammed rejected was a Trinity consisting of the Father, Jesus and Mary:

Then Allah will say: 'Jesus, son of Mary, did you ever say to mankind: "Worship me and my Mother as gods beside Allah?" '

The relationship between the Father and the Son is thought of as a purely physical relationship:

He is the Creator of the heavens and the earth. How should He have a son when he had no consort?

Never has Allah begotten a son, nor is there any other god beside him.

The Christian rejects these ideas as vigorously as the Moslem. Therefore, if you reject the Christian understanding of Jesus on these grounds, you are simply rejecting a misunderstanding which the Christian rejects as strongly as you do.

It may be, however, that in the end we must move from the details of the picture of Christ in the Qur'an and the Gospels and talk about fundamental assumptions.
▷ The original disciples of Jesus were as firmly convinced as any Moslem that God is one. This was their basic creed, their basic assumption. However, through their contact with Jesus over a period of three years they were gradually forced by what they saw and heard and experienced to *revise* their understanding of the oneness of God. They did not *reject* it; they simply revised their idea of 'oneness' in the light of the inescapable evidence which confronted them. If you are not willing even to consider the possibility of revising your assumption about the oneness of God in the light of the evidence of the life of Jesus, then the discussion must turn on some of the problems involved in insisting on the literal oneness of God. (See further Book Two, Question Two, 'Who or what is God?')

▷ If you accept the Qur'an as the Word of God, you will not be willing simply to *supplement* the Qur'an's picture of Jesus with what the Gospels say about him, because the Qur'an contains many explicit *rejections* of the divinity of Jesus:

Unbelievers are those that say: 'Allah is the Messiah, the son of Mary.' For the Messiah himself said: 'Children of Israel, serve Allah, my Lord and your Lord.' He that worships other gods besides Allah shall be forbidden Paradise and shall be cast into the fire of Hell. None shall help the evil-doers.
   Unbelievers are those that say: 'Allah is one of three.' There is but one God. If they do not desist from so saying, those of them that disbelieve shall be sternly punished.
   Will they not turn to Allah in repentance and seek forgiveness of Him? He is forgiving and merciful.
   The Messiah, the son of Mary, was no more than an apostle: other apostles passed away before him. His mother was a saintly woman. They both ate earthly food.
   See how We make plain to them Our revelations. See how they ignore the truth.

The discussion at this point, therefore, must turn on the question: How do we know what is the word of God? How can we know whether the Qur'an or the Bible is the Word of God? (See further BOOK ONE, especially pp. 12–30 and 31–39.)

ANSWER 4

"He was a man and nothing more"

This is to say, Jesus was simply a man. He was not divine in the sense that he shared the nature of a supernatural God. And he was not a created being from heaven. He may have been a very exceptional person, and he may help us to find the meaning of life. But he was not in any sense more than an ordinary human being.

Hugh Schonfield explains the Christian belief as being the result of

. . . the intrusion into early Christianity of a pagan assessment of his worth in terms of deity.

In spite of this he is able to see some deeper meaning in the person of Jesus:

We find in him the symbol both of the martyrdom and the aspirations of man, and therefore we must cling to him as the embodiment of an assurance that our life has meaning and purpose.

Paul van Buren interprets the life of Jesus through the concept of 'freedom':

Jesus of Nazareth was a singular individual. His characteristics seem to have impressed his followers so that he stands out as a remarkably free man in the records of remembered parable, saying or incident, and in the way in which the early Christian community spoke of him . . .

He followed the religious rites and obligations of his people, but he also felt free to disregard them. In miracle stories he is even presented mythologically as being free from the limitations of natural forces.

He was called rabbi, teacher, but his teaching broke down the limitations of this title . . . He simply spoke and acted with the authority of a singular freedom.

The content of his teaching reveals this same freedom . . . Perhaps the most radical expression of this freedom is found in an incident in which Jesus forgave a sick man his sins, and then demonstrated his right to do so by healing him . . . His freedom, finally, is evident in his making no claims for himself. He seems to have been so free of any need for status that he was able to resist all attempts by others to convey status on him . . .

If we would define Jesus by his freedom, however, we must emphasize its positive character. He was free from anxiety and the need to establish his own identity, but was above all free for his neighbour . . . He was free to be compassionate for his neighbour, whoever that neighbour might be, without regard to himself . . .

We have summed up the characteristics of Jesus around the one concept, freedom . . .

POINTS TO CONSIDER ABOUT THIS ANSWER

If you give this kind of answer, you are still   faced with the further question: how was it

that the early Christians came to believe that he was more than an ordinary man?

▷ If the Gospels do give a substantially reliable account of his life, what do you make of his claims about himself? In the final analysis there are only two possible answers:

either he was *deceived* and *misled* about his own identity; he was wrong about his claims, but did not know it. Therefore, at best he was mentally unbalanced, at worst he was out of his mind, completely mad.

or he *deceived* and *misled* others consciously and deliberately; he was wrong about his claims, and he knew it; but he spoke and acted in this way to get people to believe in his teaching and in what he stood for. Therefore, at best he was a teacher with ideals, who used unscrupulous methods; at worst he was a dishonest rogue.

▷ If the Gospels are not a reliable account of the life of Jesus, how are we to account for the distortion? The first Gospel was probably written 30 to 40 years after the death of Jesus; and the process of distortion must already have begun at this stage. There are three possible answers:

either the disciples and/or the writers were *deceived* and *misled*; they completely misunderstood Jesus themselves, and passed on their misunderstanding to others.

BUT: are we to imagine that Jesus spent the best part of three years with the disciples and allowed them to misunderstand him so completely?

And how can we explain this misunderstanding in the light of the vast difference between Jewish beliefs about the one God and pagan beliefs about many gods? The first disciples were all Palestinian Jews; is it likely that they would make Jesus out to be a demi-god?

or the disciples and/or the writers were *deceiving* and *misleading* their readers deliberately, although they may have had the best of motives. Somewhere along the line there were those who knew that Jesus was an ordinary man, but they made him out to be more than a man in order to convince others of the importance of his message.

BUT: how could a religion based on a lie, or even on an 'honest' deception make so much of truthfulness and honesty?

And what possible motive could they have had? Jews would find it very difficult to accept a new understanding of the oneness of God. And non-Jews would not easily accept the claims about the uniqueness of Jesus.

or the disciples and/or the writers were not misled or misleading; it is *we* who are misled if we read the Gospels as a straightforward account of what Jesus said and did. The Gospels tell us about the inward *experience* and *faith* of the first disciples, and cannot be taken as reliable evidence about the *events* behind that faith.

BUT: if we are to be agnostic about what it was that created the faith of the disciples, Christian faith ceases to be faith in the Jesus of history, and becomes faith in the faith of the first disciples. And why not carry the agnosticism one stage further and be agnostic about the *faith* of the disciples as well as the *events*?

Sooner or later the discussion must turn on basic assumptions rather than on detailed points of interpretation. One of the basic assumptions which is evident in answers of this kind is that a 'God-man' is inconceivable and incredible.

Hugh Schonfield sets out to examine the evidence about Jesus without any bias or prejudice. In his Introduction to *The Passover Plot* he begins with a claim to be unbiassed and unprejudiced:

Most books about him (Jesus) have been devotional, apologetic or polemical, and I wished mine to be none of these. What I aimed at was to shed all dispositions to make use of Jesus and allow him from his own time to explain himself to me.

But on the very next page he writes:

The traditional portraiture no longer satisfies; it is too baffling in its apparent contradiction of the terms of our earthly existence. The God-man of Christianity is increasingly incredible, yet it is not easy to break with centuries of authoritative instruction and devout faith, and there remains embedded deep in the subconscious a strong sense of the supernatural inherited from remote ages.

One of his basic assumptions, therefore, is that the Christian interpretation of Jesus can be safely ruled out from the start because it no longer satisfies and appears increasingly incredible.

Joel Carmichael, in his book *The Death of Jesus*, begins with a claim to be objective:

My attitude throughout is purely historical.

But a little later he declares his presuppositions:

The international cultic transformation of perspective involved in the magnification of Jesus was accompanied by the external, historical change of perspective due to the growing and ultimately unbridged schism between the new sect and Judaism.
  This theme is basic in any study of Christian origins . . .
  This will give us our cardinal criterion:
  Anything that conflicts with this transformation or perspective is likely to be true.
  That is, any fragment we can manage to isolate that runs counter to the prevailing Gospel tendency of exalting Jesus, or preaching his universality, and of emphasising his originality, will be regarded as *ipso facto* probable (other things, of course, being equal).

Even as a historian he cannot approach the enquiry without any assumptions. In this case he declares that it was the Christians who made Jesus God; therefore none of the evidence of the New Testament can be taken at its face value.

Paul van Buren indicates that he begins his study accepting the basic assumptions of 'secular man'. His interpretation is determined by the methods of linguistic analysis:

How can the Christian who is himself a secular man understand his faith in a secular way? . . . The answer will be reached by analysing what a man means when he uses the language of faith, when he repeats the earliest Christian confession: 'Jesus is Lord'.

The question is whether a Christian is to be

Dr Hugh Schonfield, author of The Passover Plot.

distinguished from an 'unbeliever' by a different logic or thinking . . . We shall conduct this study on the assumption that 'being a Christian' does not deny one's involvement in the secular world and its way of thinking. This assumption will govern our attempt to understand the Christian conviction that 'Jesus is Lord'.

He admits that Jesus is not unique in having freedom:

Having spoken of him as an exceptionally liberated individual, we should point out that we might say this of other men.

If you approach the Gospels with assumptions of this kind, no amount of detailed study of the Gospels is likely to make you change your mind. It is the assumption itself which needs to be tested and challenged. (See further BOOK TWO, Question Two 'Who or what is God?' and Question Three, 'What is man?')

ANSWER 5

"He was only a man
—but also a revelation
of 'God'"

This is to say, he was an ordinary man; he was not related personally to a supernatural God, for no such God exists. However, if we redefine the word 'God', we can see in Jesus a revelation of the true meaning of 'God'.

F. C. Happold:

What the early Christians saw in Jesus, implicitly if not explicitly, was a full and perfect pattern of divinity, so far as divinity could be shown forth in man. This divinity, moreover, was inherent in each one of them. For Jesus was Representative Man, Archetypal Man, Man as he might be if he could become that which in his essential nature he really is: or, as a Hindu would put it, if he could realize his Greater Self.

John Robinson:

Jesus himself said in so many words, 'If I claim anything for myself, do not beleive me'.

It is, indeed, an open question whether Jesus ever claimed to be the Son of God, let alone God . . .

We cannot be sure what titles Jesus claimed . . .

Jesus makes no claims for himself in his own right and at the same time makes the most tremendous claims about what God is doing through him and uniquely through him . . .

Jesus never claims to be God, personally: yet he claims to bring God, completely.

It is in Jesus, and Jesus alone, that there is nothing of self to be seen, but solely the ultimate, unconditional love of God. It is as he emptied himself utterly of himself that he became the carrier of 'the name which is above every name', and that glory is simply Love.

For it is in making himself nothing, in his utter self-surrender to others in love, that he discloses and lays bare the Ground of man's being as Love.

What is Christ for us today?

Jesus is 'the man for others', the one in whom Love has completely taken over, the one who is utterly open to, and united with, the Ground of his being . . . For at this point, of love 'to the uttermost', we encounter *God*, the ultimate 'depth' of our being, the unconditional in the conditioned. This is what the New Testament means by saying that 'God was in Christ' and that 'what God was the Word was'. Because Christ was utterly and completely 'the man for others', because he *was* love, he was 'one with the Father', because 'God is love'.

POINTS TO CONSIDER ABOUT THIS ANSWER

These answers are based on assumptions about the meaning of the word 'God' which are clearly expressed.

F. C. Happold begins with an understanding

of the meaning of the word 'God' which is very different from the Christian understanding. He assumes that all the religions have basically the same vision of 'God' and 'man', even though they use different words and symbols.

Eternal and essential God-man-unity; this is what these men saw and what they were determined to express, even though, with their inherited idea of God, it seemed to involve contradictions. In doing so they expressed the supreme significance of the Christian revelation. For the Incarnation of Jesus Christ was not only a diaphany of the Divine, but also a diaphany of the human.

Though they express it in different ways according to their different theologies and philosophies, the mystics of all religions are at one in asserting the inherent divinity of man's real self. This inner deity is, however, hidden. It exists at the level of human existence as a potentiality. For it to become an actuality a 'divine birth' must take place in the soul, so that a man is raised to a higher state of consciousness. In Christianity this divine birth is thought of as the birth of Jesus Christ, the eternal Son or Logos (Word) of God, in the centre of the soul.

John Robinson shows clearly that his starting-point is the assumption that 'God' is not to be thought of as a supernatural being:

As long as God and man are thought of as two 'beings', each with distinct natures, one from 'the other side' and one from 'this side', then it is impossible to create out of them more than a God-man, a divine visitant from 'out there' who chooses in every respect to live like the natives. The supernaturalist view of the Incarnation can never really rid itself of the idea of the prince who appears in the guise of the beggar. However genuinely destitute the beggar may be, he *is* a prince; and that in the end is what matters.

If you begin with assumptions of this kind, the details of the Gospel narratives will be irrelevant. The discussion must therefore hinge on the meaning of the word 'God'. (See further BOOK TWO, Question Two, 'Who or what is God?')

These answers are based on the assumption that the truth about Jesus can be expressed in many different ways, depending on the standpoint of the individual.

F. C. Happold believes that statements of Christian belief, like statements of any kind of belief, express intuitions arising out of personal experience:

What may not be able to be established as either scientifically or historically true, may be regarded as *mythically* and *dogmatically* true.

When examined objectively, dogma is seen to be a complex of mythological, symbolic, metaphysical, psychological, mystical and, in the Christian creeds, historical elements. It is a translation into the terms of the intellect of intuitions which have been apprehended mystically, psychologically and intuitively. It is thus a particular sort of truth demanding a particular sort of language, which, like every other sort of language, has to be learnt, if it is to be rightly understood.

John Robinson understands the language of the New Testament in terms of 'myth':

But suppose the whole notion of 'a God' who 'visits' the earth in the person of 'his Son' is as mythical as the prince in the fairy story? Suppose the Christian myth (the invasion of 'this side' by 'the other side')—as opposed to the Christmas history (the birth of the man Jesus of Nazareth)—has to go? Are we prepared for that? Or are we to cling here to this last vestige of the mythological or metaphysical world-view as the only garb in which to clothe the story with power to touch the imagination? Cannot perhaps the supernaturalist scheme survive at least as part of the 'magic' of Christmas?

Yes, indeed, it can survive—as myth. For myth has its perfectly legitimate, and indeed profoundly important, place. The myth is there to indicate the significance of the events, the divine depth of the history.

Assumptions of this kind must be discussed on their own, for they have nothing to do with the Gospel accounts of the life of Jesus. What is at stake is our understanding of what truth is. (See further BOOK ONE.)

"He was both man and God: he was the Son of God"

PROBLEMS AND QUESTIONS

Having examined other possible answers to the basic question, we must now return to option one, the Biblical Christian answer, and look at some of the main questions and objections raised.

Can we be really certain that Jesus actually lived?

The following are the four main witnesses outside the New Testament to the historicity of Jesus.

Pliny, a Roman pro-consul in Bithynia (Asia Minor), writing to the Emperor Trajan in AD 110 about the way in which he has been dealing with Christians:

This is the course that I have adopted in the case of those brought before me as Christians. I ask them if they are Christians. If they admit it I repeat the question a second and a third time, threatening capital punishment; if they persist I sentence them to death. For I do not doubt that, whatever kind of crime it may be to which they have confessed, their pertinacity and inflexible obstinacy should certainly be punished. There were others who displayed a like madness and whom I reserved to be sent to Rome, since they were Roman citizens.

Thereupon the usual result followed: the very fact of my dealing with the question led to a wider spread of the charge, and a great variety of cases were brought before me. An anonymous pamphlet was issued, containing many names. All who denied that they were or had been Christians I considered should be discharged, because they called upon the gods at my dictation and did reverence, with incense and wine, to your image which I had ordered to be brought forward for this purpose, together with the statues of the deities; and especially because they cursed Christ, a thing which, it is said, genuine Christians cannot be induced to do. Others named by the informer first said that they were Christians and then denied it; declaring that they had been but were so no longer, some having recanted three years or more before and one or two as long ago as twenty years. They all worshipped your image and the statues of the gods and cursed Christ.

But they declared that the sum of their guilt or error had amounted only to this, that on an appointed day they had been accustomed to meet before daybreak, and recite a hymn antiphonally to Christ, as to a god, and to bind themselves by an oath, not for the commission of any crime but to abstain from theft, robbery, adultery and breach of faith, and not to deny a deposit when it was claimed. . . .

Tacitus, the Roman historian, writing in about AD 115 about Nero's persecution of Christians in the year AD 64:

But all the endeavours of men, all the emperor's largesse and the propitiations of the gods, did not suffice to allay the scandal or banish the belief that the fire had been ordered. And so, to get rid of this rumour, Nero set up as the culprits and punished with the utmost refinement of cruelty a class hated for their abominations, who are commonly called Christians. Christus, from whom their name is derived, was executed at the hands of the procurator Pontius Pilate in the reign of Tiberius. Checked for the moment, this pernicious superstition again broke out, not only in Judaea, the source of the evil, but even in Rome, that receptacle for everything that is sordid and degrading from every quarter of the globe, which there finds a following.

Suetonius, the Roman historian, writing in about AD 120 in his *Life of Claudius* (the Emperor from 41–54). It is probable that 'Chrestus' is a confusion of 'Christus' (Christ).

Since the Jews were continually making disturbances at the instigation of Chrestus, he (Claudius) expelled them from Rome.

This probably refers to quarrels between Jews and Christian teachers about Jesus.

Josephus, the Jewish historian, writing about AD 93 or 94 in his *Antiquities of the Jews* (this version is based on the Greek text, which dates from the fourth century):

About this time there arose Jesus, a wise man, if indeed it be lawful to call him a man. For he was a doer of wonderful deeds, and a teacher of men who gladly receive the truth. He drew to himself many both of the Jews and of the Gentiles. He was the Christ; and when Pilate, on the indictment of the principal men among us, had condemned him to the cross, those who loved him at the first did not cease to do so, for he appeared to them again alive on the third day, the divine prophets having foretold these and ten thousand wonderful things about him. And even to this day the race of Christians, who are named after him, has not died out.

Josephus was not a Christian, and some scholars have argued that some clauses (e.g. 'he was the Christ') could not have been written by Josephus, and must have been interpolated in an early text by a Christian. But others, including scholars who have no Christian bias, see no reason for doubting that Josephus could have written these words. They argue that this is exactly how a slightly cynical Jew might refer to Christian beliefs about Jesus.

Further light has been shed on this text by Professor Shlomo Pines of the Hebrew University in Jerusalem, who has discovered an Arabic version of the same text which he believes to be older than the Greek one. It was found in a church history written by Bishop Agapius, an Arab Bishop in Baghdad. This is what the Arabic text says:

At this time there was a wise man who was called Jesus. And his conduct was good and (he) was known to be virtuous. And many people from among the Jews and from the other nations became his disciples. Pilate condemned him to be crucified and to die.

And those who had become his disciples did not abandon his discipleship. They reported

---

The Colosseum in Rome, where 45,000 citizens could watch the entertainments. Here thousands of Christians were martyred for their faith.

Coins showing the heads of the Roman Emperors Claudius and Nero. Both had to deal with troubles involving Jewish and Christian groups.

that he had appeared to them three days after his crucifixion and that he was alive. Accordingly he was perhaps the Messiah of whom the prophets have recounted wonders.

Professor Pines believes that medieval Christian censorship was probably responsible for the differences between the two versions:

The Arabic version is less Christian in character than the traditional Greek one. Because of this it may be an earlier version than the traditional one.

In another passage in the *Antiquities*, Josephus writes about the martyrdom of James, the brother of Jesus:

(Ananus) assembled the sanhedrin of the judges, and brought before them the brother of Jesus, who was called Christ, whose name was James, and some others, and when he had formed an accusation against them as breakers of the law, he delivered them to be stoned.

Roderic Dunkerley, in his book *Beyond the Gospels* examines all the evidence about Jesus from contemporary sources outside the New Testament and comes to this conclusion:

In none of these various testimonies to the fact of Christ is there any slightest hint or idea that he was not a real historical person . . . Indeed it has been argued—and I think very rightly—that myth theories of the beginnings of Christianity are modern speculative hypotheses motivated by unreasoning prejudice and dislike. 'It would never enter anyone's head,' says Merezhovsky, 'to ask whether Jesus had lived, unless before asking the question the mind had been darkened by the wish that he had not lived.'

⚠ Why is there so little about the virgin birth in the rest of the New Testament?

The only direct evidence for belief in the virgin birth in the New Testament is contained in the two passages from Luke and Matthew. If the belief is important, why do the other Gospels not record the story? And if no other book in the New Testament speaks of it, does this not mean that the belief was not well known in the early period?

▷ From the very nature of the case, we would not expect the story to be common knowledge in the early days of the church.

At first only Mary and Joseph would have known the circumstances of the conception of Jesus. They would hardly be likely to tell the story to others inside or outside the family.

Joseph must have died at some time before Jesus began his public ministry. Mary would have no compelling motive for publishing the story, since she herself seems to have had doubts about him during this period. Luke gives the impression that Mary kept the secret to herself, and that he heard the story about Jesus' birth and childhood from her own mouth:

. . . and all who heard it wondered at what the

An ancient icon of the Virgin Mary, encrusted with pearls and precious stones.

The story might therefore have remained a secret tradition, known only to a small number.

▷ There are hints in other parts of the New Testament that something was known about the unusual circumstances of his birth.

When the Jews objected to the way in which Jesus called himself 'the Son', they taunted him with these words:

We were not born of fornication; we have one Father, even God.

The implication may well be 'We were not born of fornication—*as you were.*'

Paul speaks of the entrance of Jesus into the world in these words:

When the time had fully come, God sent forth his Son, born of woman, born under the law . . .

▷ There are two possible conclusions we can draw from the scarcity of references to the virgin birth:

either the story was invented as a way of adding to the dignity of Jesus, but it was not widely known or accepted, or regarded as important in the early days.

or it could simply underline the general impression we get from the rest of the New Testament that Mary is completely overshadowed by Jesus and that the circumstances of his death and resurrection were regarded as being far more important than his birth.

shepherds told them. But Mary kept all these things, pondering them in her heart.
And he (Jesus) went down with them and came to Nazareth, and was obedient to them; and his mother kept all these things in her heart.

In the early days of the church, the story of the death and resurrection of Jesus would have overshadowed the story of his birth.

⚠ What is the rightful place of Mary in Christian faith and devotion?

If Mary played such a significant role in the coming of Jesus into the world and in his early life, what place should she have in Christian faith and devotion today?

Nicholas Zernov, writing about Eastern Orthodox beliefs:

Among these saints a unique place is reserved for the Mother of God—the Virgin Mary. The long process of purification and enlightenment of the Jewish race so vividly described in the Old Testament reached its culmination in the Theotokos (Mary). In her the faith and heroism of many generations of the Chosen People found fulfilment. She accepted with humility the challenge of the Annunciation. During the lifetime of her Son she kept in the background, but she presided over the assembly of apostles on the day of Pentecost, when the new period in the history of mankind was inaugurated by the descent of the Holy Spirit. 'Warm Veneration of the Theotokos is the soul of Orthodox piety', writes Fr. Bulgakov. Her name is constantly invoked in both liturgical and personal prayers, she is loved, not only as the Mother of Christ, but also as the Mother of mankind, for she embraces in her charity the entire human family of which her Son is the sole Redeemer.

▷ The first thing to note is how Mary was addressed by the angel at the time of his visitation, and how she thought of herself. The angel addressed her in these words:

Hail, O favoured one, the Lord is with you! . . . Do not be afraid, Mary, for you have found favour with God. And behold, you will conceive in your womb and bear a son, and you shall call his name Jesus . . . (Revised Standard Version)

Greetings, most favoured one . . . (New English Bible)

Rejoice, so highly favoured! . . . (Jerusalem Bible)

There is no justification for the translation 'full of grace', or for the idea that Mary is a means by which God gives grace to men. The greeting is explained by the later sentence, 'You have found favour with God.'

Mary responded to the angel's message:

Behold I am the handmaid of the Lord; let it be to me according to your word.

▷ Some incidents are recorded in which Jesus seems to play down the human and physical relationship between himself and his mother:

And his mother and his brothers came; and standing outside they sent to him and called him. And a crowd was sitting about him; and they said to him, 'Your mother and your brothers are outside, asking for you.' And he replied, 'Who are my mother and my brothers?' And looking around on those who sat about him, he said, 'Here are my mother and my brothers! Whoever does the will of God is my brother, and sister, and mother.'

A woman in the crowd raised her voice and said to him, 'Blessed is the womb that bore you, and the breasts that you sucked!' But he said, 'Blessed rather are those who hear the word of God and keep it!'

At the wedding at Cana, Mary seems to be wanting to impress her will on Jesus and he replies:

O woman, what have you to do with me?

When he hung on the cross, he committed Mary to the care of John the disciple:

. . . he said to his mother, 'Woman, behold your son!' Then he said to the disciple, 'Behold your mother!'

In these last two incidents he addressed her as 'woman', which would not have been an insult, but a title of respect. If, however, he had wanted to emphasize the mother-son

Pope Paul gives a televised address at the shrine of the Virgin Mary at Fatima.

relationship, it would have been very natural for him to address her as 'mother'. It seems that Jesus had to make it clear to Mary— gently but firmly—that the relationship between them could not always be the ordinary mother-son relationship.

▷ The only other reference to Mary outside the Gospels is in Acts, where she is described as joining with the other disciples in prayer:

All these with one accord devoted themselves to prayer, together with the women and Mary the mother of Jesus, and with his brothers.

There is no suggestion that Mary was presiding over the gathering, as Zernov claims.

In the context of the early chapters of Acts this can only mean that Mary joined with the other disciples in prayer to God *through* the risen Jesus, or *to* the risen Jesus himself.

▷ One further point. In the book of Revelation, in which John describes his vision of heaven there is no reference to Mary. There is no suggestion that Mary has already received a place of special honour in heaven, or that she is in any sense to be regarded as a mediator between men and God.

So perhaps we come nearest to the mind of Mary herself, and of Jesus, if we give her the simple but honourable title she herself used—'the handmaid of the Lord'.

⚠ Why is there so little in the Gospels about the early life of Jesus?

The Jewish Encyclopedia:

Perhaps the most remarkable thing about the life of Jesus as presented in the Gospels is the utter silence about its earlier phases.

▷ The only details given in the Gospels are these.

Joseph and Mary took Jesus to Egypt while he was still a baby because of the threat to his life from Herod. After the death of Herod, they returned to Nazareth, and it was here that he was brought up (Matthew 2: 13–15).

Jesus had brothers and sisters who were born to Mary and Joseph (this is the most natural and obvious interpretation of the references to the 'brothers' of Jesus):

Many who heard him (Jesus) were astonished, saying, 'Where did this man get all this? . . . Is not this the carpenter, the son of Mary and brother of James and Joses and Judas and Simon, and are not his sisters here with us?

Similarly, Paul speaks of

. . . James, the Lord's brother . . .

The interpretation that the 'brothers' were in fact cousins and not blood-brothers first appears in Christian writings in the third century. This tradition seems to have been associated with the belief that Mary remained a virgin after her marriage to Joseph and after the birth of Jesus; but there is no basis for this belief in the New Testament itself.

Jesus first visited Jerusalem at the age of twelve. After a long search his parents found him 'in the temple, sitting among the teachers, listening to them and asking them questions' (Luke 2: 41–51)

Joseph, his foster-father, was a carpenter, and it appears that Jesus learned this trade from him. Joseph must have died before Jesus left home for his public ministry. Being the eldest son, Jesus would have had the responsibility for the home (Matthew 13: 55).

▷ Our only other source of information about the early life of Jesus is the so-called apocryphal Gospels.

Roderic Dunkerley:

As regards the conventionally called 'apocryphal Gospels' . . . it does not take very much examination to convince us that they are almost entirely fiction not fact. They deal mostly with the nativity and boyhood of Jesus on the one hand, and with his passion and resurrection on the other. Many fantastic miracles are attributed to the child Jesus, as for example that he made birds of clay and then they flew away, and again that another boy who accidentally ran against him dropped down and died . . .

But we cannot rule out the possibility that here and there some small points of authentic tradition may have survived amidst all the fiction and fantasy . . . Dean Farrar in his *Life of Christ* quoted the following charming little tale and thought it might be based on fact:

Now in the month of Adar, Jesus assembled

the boys as if he were their king; they strewed their garments on the ground and he sat upon them. Then they put on his head a crown wreathed of flowers and like attendants waiting on a king they stood in order before him on his right hand and on his left. And whoever passed that way the boys took him by force saying, Come hither and adore the King and then proceed upon thy way.

This is quite different from the usual grotesque narratives and is something that might quite easily have happened—and been remembered and retold. But it cannot be more than an interesting possibility.

▷ If we ask why the writers of the Gospels do not tell us more about the early life of Jesus, the simplest answer is that they were not intending to write full biographies of Jesus. Their main concern was with his public ministry, his death and resurrection.

⚠ How trustworthy are reports of the character of Jesus which were written by his friends and admirers?

The point raised is that reports about his character are bound to be prejudiced because they were written by admirers who idolized him, and who would not have been able to see his faults.

▷ The Gospels say that the disciples were with Jesus for the best part of three years. And these Gospels were written either by some of the disciples or by others who were acquainted with them. We are dealing therefore with the testimony of men who knew him intimately, and not with casual acquaintances. John claims, for example, to be writing about someone he knew very well:

That which was from the beginning, which we have heard, which we have seen with our eyes, which we have looked upon and touched with our hands . . .

▷ The disciples would have been brought up to believe that *all* men are sinners:

God looks down from heaven
  upon the sons of men
to see if there are any that are wise,
  that seek after God.
They have all fallen away;
  they are all alike depraved;
There is none that does good,
  no, not one.

All we like sheep have gone astray;
  we have turned every one to his own way . . .

The disciples would have had to have some very good reason for claiming that Jesus was an exception to this rule.

▷ None of the New Testament writers goes out of his way to paint an impressive picture of the character of Jesus. All that we learn about his character is from his actions and his words; there are no passages which set out to describe what kind of person he was. In the two cases where they speak of his sinlessness, they do so almost as an aside:

. . . . Christ also suffered for you, leaving you an example, that you should follow in his steps. He committed no sin; no guile was found on his lips. When he was reviled, he did not revile in return . . .

You know that he appeared to take away sins, and in him there is no sin.

▷ The Gospel writers also attempt to give some idea of what Jesus' critics and enemies thought of him. These were some of the accusations they brought against him:

  blasphemy:

  Who can forgive sins but God alone?

  keeping bad company:

  Why does he eat with tax collectors and sinners?

  that his disciples were not strict enough in their religious observances:

  Why do your disciples not fast?

  that his disciples broke the sabbath:

  Why are they (the disciples) doing what is not lawful on the sabbath? (They were going against a ruling of the scribes, but not against the Old Testament itself.)

The Gospel writers make no deliberate attempt to defend Jesus from any of these charges. They simply leave their accounts of his actions and words to speak for themselves.

▷ If the disciples and the writers *were* conscious of weaknesses or faults in his character, they have been very clever in suppressing them—and very much cleverer than the followers and admirers of other great men have been.

▷ None of the founders and leaders of the great religions —e.g. Mohammed or Buddha or Confucius—ever claimed that he was perfect, or sinless; and their followers generally have never made this claim for them.

⚠ Why did Jesus appear at times to conceal his identity?

Why was he so indirect in his claims about himself? If he really was God the Son, why did he not say so directly and openly from the beginning, so as to leave no shadow of doubt in people's minds? When some *did* think of him as 'the Christ' or as 'the Son of God', why did he tell them not to tell others?

And whenever the unclean spirits beheld him, they fell down before him and cried out, 'You are the Son of God.' And he strictly ordered them not to make him known.

And he (Jesus) asked them (the disciples), 'But who do you say that I am?' Peter answered him, 'You are the Christ.' And he charged them to tell no one about him.

▷ *A political reason:* Jesus would have been well aware of the confused and misleading ideas about the Messiah which were circulating at the time (e.g. the idea of the warrior king who would lead the Jews to drive out the Romans, or the heavenly Son of man who would descend from the clouds in glory).

If he had repeatedly used titles like 'Messiah', he would have identified himself in the eyes of the people and the Roman authorities with the extreme nationalists, and he might well have been taken as a purely political figure.

▷ *A theological reason:* Jesus would also have been aware of the Jewish emphasis on the oneness of God: 'The Lord our God is one Lord . . .' If he had made direct and unmistakeable claims from the beginning, his hearers might not have been willing even to give him a hearing. A certain indirectness would force people to think for themselves and to come gradually to understand the full implications of what he claimed. However, we must add, that although the claims of Jesus may seem very indirect and subtle to us today, they would have sounded *less* so to the well-taught Jew who heard him. No Jew would fail to see what was implied when

Jesus claimed authority to forgive sins—he would immediately accuse him of blasphemy.

▷ *A moral reason:* when Jesus spoke indirectly about himself, he was not simply encouraging his hearers to think with their minds. He was at the same time presenting a challenge to their wills and their consciences. On one occasion he refused to be more direct simply because he could see that his questioners were ignoring the moral challenge in what they already knew.

As he was walking in the temple, the chief priests and the scribes and the elders came to him, and they said to him, 'By what authority are you doing these things, or who gave you this authority to do them?' Jesus said to them, 'I will ask you a question; answer me, and I will tell you by what authority I do these things. Was the baptism of John from heaven or from men? Answer me.' And they argued with one another, 'If we say, "From heaven," he will say, "Why then did you not believe him?" But shall we say, "From men"?'—they were afraid of the people, for all held that John was a real prophet. So they answered Jesus, 'We do not know.' And Jesus said to them, 'Neither will I tell you by what authority I do these things.'

Jesus' claims so enraged the people of Nazareth that they took him forcibly to a nearby cliff, 'to throw him headlong'.

▷ *The time factor:* when the disciples came to realize that he was the Christ, the Son of God, he told them not to tell anyone openly:

And he asked them, 'But who do you say that I am?' Peter answered him, 'You are the Christ.' And he charged them to tell no one about him.
  And he began to teach them that the Son of man must suffer many things . . . and be killed, and after three days rise again.

Very soon after this three of the disciples witnessed the transfiguration, and Jesus gave a similar command:

As they were coming down the mountain, he charged them to tell no one what they had seen, until the Son of man should have risen from the dead. So they kept the matter to themselves, questioning what the rising from the dead meant.

This suggests that Jesus expected that what was hidden and obscure *during* his lifetime would be proclaimed openly to all *after* his death and resurrection.

▷ *Direct answers:* on some occasions when he was presented with a direct question, he gave a direct answer:

The high priest said to him, 'I adjure you by the living God, tell us if you are the Christ, the Son of God.' Jesus said to him, 'You have said so . . .' (or 'the words are yours', New English Bible) . . . Then the high priest tore his robes, and said, 'He has uttered blasphemy . . .'

⚠ Are all the miracle stories equally important and relevant?

Should we not distinguish between the different kinds of miracles, and be prepared to admit that some are less unlikely than others? For example, is it not easier to believe some of the healing miracles because of what we are now finding out about the power of mind over body? This kind of miracle presents fewer problems to the scientific mind than the feeding of the 5,000.

▷ This approach still leaves us with the questions: how are we to define what is a 'likely' or 'credible' or 'suitable' miracle, and what would be 'unlikely', or 'incredible' or 'inappropriate'? It is very hard to draw these dividing lines, and once we start drawing them the critic has every right to say, 'Why do you stop there? Why don't you exclude more?'

▷ Everything depends on our assumptions about God and the universe: is he or is he not the Creator and Sustainer of the universe? Is he or is he not the infinite and personal God who wants to demonstrate his existence and his character, and to act in order to meet the needs of men? If we begin with the assumption that he exists, and that this is what he is like, then our question about the miracles becomes: is this miracle story consistent with this idea of God—or is it not? If we reject this assumption, or if we refuse

to commit ourselves to it explicitly, our discussion should turn on assumptions rather than on the miracle stories themselves. (See further BOOK TWO, Question Two, 'Who

The Pool of Bethesda, with its five porticos, has recently been discovered deep below the level of present-day Jerusalem. Here Jesus healed the man crippled for 38 years.

or what is God?' and Question Four, 'What kind of universe do we live in?')

▷ This question is often based on the assumption that if we do not insist that all the miracles really happened, then it will be easier for the doubter to believe. But it is hard to reconcile this assumption with the realism of the Gospels, which suggest that there was little difference between the effects of the 'extraordinary' miracles and the 'more ordinary' ones. Many of them played an important part in bringing individuals and groups to believe in Jesus and accept his claims about himself. But there is no suggestion that they persuaded vast numbers of people; and sometimes we are given no idea of whether or not they led the people concerned to believe. All the Gospels speak of the suspicion and ill-feeling and opposition aroused by some of the miracles. And one miracle, the raising of Lazarus from death, led to the final plot to kill Jesus.

Mark shows that right from the beginning the miracles of Jesus aroused opposition:

And he looked around at them with anger, grieved at their hardness of heart, and said to the man, 'Stretch out your hand.' He stretched it out, and his hand was restored. The Pharisees went out, and immediately held counsel with the Herodians against him, how to destroy him.

John notes the effects of six of the seven miracles he records:

—Turning the water into wine:

This, the first of his signs, Jesus did at Cana in Galilee, and manifested his glory; and his disciples believed in him.

—The healing of the son of the official at Capernaum:

He (the father) himself believed, and all his household.

—The healing of the paralysed man at the pool in Jerusalem:

This was why the Jews sought all the more to kill him, because he not only broke the sabbath, but also called God his Father, making himself equal with God.

—The feeding of the 5,000:

When the people saw the sign which he had done they said, 'This is indeed the prophet who is to come into the world!' Perceiving then that they were about to come and take him by force and make him king, Jesus withdrew again.

In the discussion which followed when the crowd found Jesus the next day, he made some very big claims for himself—e.g. 'I am the bread which came down from heaven.' This was the reaction:

Many of his disciples, when they heard it, said, 'This is a hard saying; who can listen to it?' . . . After this many of his disciples drew back and no longer went about with him.

—The healing of the man blind from birth:

They (the religious authorities) cast him out. Jesus heard that they had cast him out, and having found him he said, 'Do you believe in the Son of man?' He answered, 'And who is he, sir, that I may believe in him?' Jesus said to him. 'You have seen him, and it is he who speaks to you.' He said, 'Lord, I believe' and he worshipped him.

—The raising of Lazarus from the dead:

Many of the Jews therefore, who had come with Mary and had seen what he did, believed in him; but some of them went to the Pharisees and told them what Jesus had done. So the chief priests and the Pharisees gathered the council, and said, 'What are we to do? For this man performs many signs. If we let him go on thus, everyone will believe in him . . . ' So from that day on they took counsel how to put him to death.

▷ The contrast between the miracles recorded in the Gospels and the miracles recorded in the apocryphal Gospels and the Qur'an (see p. 27) is very significant.

The Gospel of Thomas includes the following stories in which the boy Jesus works miracles largely to get himself out of awkward situations:

Now on a day, when Jesus climbed up upon an house with the children, he began to play with them: but one of the boys fell down through the door out of the upper chamber and died straightway. And when the children saw it they fled all of them, but Jesus remained alone in the house. And when the parents of the child which had died came they spake against Jesus saying: Of a truth thou madest him fall. But Jesus said: I never made him fall: nevertheless they accused him still. Jesus therefore came down from the house and stood over the dead child and cried with a loud voice, calling him by his name: Zeno, Zeno, arise and say if I made thee fall. And on a sudden he arose and said: Nay, Lord. And when his parents saw this great miracle which Jesus did, they glorified God, and worshipped Jesus.

And when Jesus was six years old, his mother sent him to draw water. And when Jesus was come unto the well there was much people there and they brake his pitcher. But he took the cloak which he had upon him and filled it with water and brought it to Mary his mother. And when his mother saw the miracle that Jesus did she kissed him and said: Lord, hearken unto me and save my son.

⚠ How could a single personality be both human and divine?

It is one thing to conceive of God as a personal Being; but it is very difficult, if not impossible, to conceive of this God uniting himself in any way with human nature. And if a man has a fully human personality, how can he at the same time be fully divine?

▷ Everything here depends on our assumptions about God and man. The Christian believes that man has been created in the image and likeness of God:

Then God said, 'Let us make man in our image, after our likeness . . .'

When God created man, he made him in the likeness of God. Male and female he created them, and blessed them, and named them Man when they were created . . . Adam . . . became the father of a son in his own likeness, after his image, and named him Seth . . .

The image of God in man has been marred and spoiled by man's rebellion against God, but it has not been obliterated or defaced completely. Even fallen man is *like God* in certain respects. There is not a total discontinuity between God and man. Godhead and humanity are not opposites. If we begin with this assumption, then we may be prepared to believe that Jesus could be both human and divine *provided* the detailed evidence for it is compelling.

If, on the other hand, we believe that God is 'the Wholly Other', who is remote and completely different from man, then there can hardly be any point of contact between them. The gulf between deity and humanity becomes too great to be bridged in a single personality.

If we interpret the oneness of God as a strictly literal oneness, no amount of detailed evidence will make us revise our ideas of what oneness could be. We may allow that in the physical world there can be different kinds of unity, like the complex unity of the atom. And we may allow that husband and wife are 'a unity' (as the writer of Genesis says). But if we insist on sticking to our assumption of a literal oneness, then it will always be inconceivable that Jesus could be anything more than a man in close touch with God.

▷ If we approach the question from a purely biblical point of view, we find that the enigma of humanity and deity combined in a single personality is already implicit in Daniel's visions of the 'son of man'. Every Jew was brought up to believe the statement Jesus used to refute Satan (Matthew 4: 10): 'You shall worship the Lord your God, and him only shall you serve. Daniel's vision of the son of man must therefore have sounded strange, if not incredible to Jewish ears:

I saw in the night visions,
and behold, with the clouds of heaven
    there came one like a son of man,
and he came to the Ancient of Days
    and was presented before him.
And to him was given dominion and glory and kingdom,
    that all peoples, nations, and languages should serve him;
his dominion is an everlasting dominion,
    which shall not pass away,
and his kingdom one that shall not be destroyed.

We may well ask: who can this 'son of man' be who is worshipped by people of all nations and languages? How can God give him the 'dominion and glory and kingdom' which belong exclusively to himself? When Jesus adopted the title 'son of man', he probably took it from these passages in Daniel.

▷ As far as the New Testament is concerned we need to look at the problem from the standpoint of the first disciples. When they first met Jesus, they were confronted by a man who was every bit as human as they were. Nothing in their experience of him during the three years of his ministry can have made them doubt his real humanity. Even when they saw his miracles, they saw them as the work of a man: '*What sort of man* is this, that even winds and sea obey him?' (Matthew 8: 27). At the same time, the combined evidence of his character, his claims and his miracles forced them to associate him more and more closely with God.

Obviously they could not have arrived at this position in an instant; and when they did, they would not have wanted (or been able) to formulate any philosophical concept of a God-man. All they could do was to say in effect, 'All the evidence points to the fact that this man Jesus is truly one of us; he is *one with us*. He must also be *one with God*, and in some sense must be God.' The New Testament writers therefore do not try to explain philosophically how a single personality could be divine and human; they simply paint a portrait of Jesus as they knew him, and use every title they can think of to identify him *both* with God *and* with man.

⚠ What is the meaning of the term 'Son of God'?

If a person who believes in Jesus can be called a 'son of God' (see BOOK TWO, p. 55) in what sense can Jesus be called '*the* Son of God?'

▷ *The Old Testament background.* In the Old Testament the metaphor of the father-son relationship is used in different ways to refer to those who have a special relationship of some kind with God.

For example, *Job* speaks of the angels as sons of God:

Where were you when I laid the
   foundations of the earth? . . .
On what were its bases sunk,
   or who laid its cornerstone,
when the morning stars sang together,
   and all the sons of God shouted for joy?

Hosea says of the people of Israel:

When Israel was a child, I loved him,
   and out of Egypt I called my son.

Israel's king is described in these words:

Thus says the Lord of hosts (to David), I took you from the pasture, from following the sheep, that you should be prince over my people Israel . . . When your days are fulfilled and you lie down with your fathers, I will raise up your son after you, who shall come forth from your body, and I will establish his kingdom . . . I will be his father, and he shall be my son. When he commits iniquity, I will chasten him with the rod of men . . .

▷ *Jesus' use of the father-son metaphor* (see the references on p. 11). In all these sayings Jesus speaks of a relationship of deep intimacy with God. And when he makes a sharp distinction between 'my Father' and 'your Father', he implies that there is something unique about his sonship; he is not merely an ordinary man who is very conscious of God.

▷ *The main ideas implied in the metaphor.* The phrase is not used to say anything about the *origin* of Jesus, the eternal Son, but rather to say something about his *relationship* with God. It does not tell us 'where he came from', because the eternal Son has always been with the Father and the Spirit; it simply tells us about his relationship with the Father. There seem to be at least three main ideas associated with the father-son relationship in the Bible:

—Likeness ('like father, like son'). In this case, the idea is that Jesus is supremely 'like God'; his character bears the closest possible resemblance to the character of God. When a person becomes a Christian, he becomes a 'son of God' or a 'child of God' in a derived sense. And the family likeness is meant to be evident in the Christian. *John* writes:

See what love the Father has given us, that we should be called children of God; and so we are. The reason why the world does not know us is that it did not know him. Beloved, we are God's children now; it does not yet appear what we shall be, but we know that when he appears we shall be like him, for we shall see him as he is.

—Knowledge. One might say that in an ordinary family, the better the father, the better he will know his son, and the better the son will know his father. This knowledge should be mutual with father and son

Father and son, both orthodox Jews, taking part in prayers at the Wailing Wall in Jerusalem. On their foreheads are phylacteries containing part of the law.

understanding and knowing each other intimately. This is the idea expressed in these words of Jesus:

I thank thee, Father, Lord of heaven and earth, that thou hast hidden these things from the wise and understanding and revealed them to babes; yea, Father, for such was thy gracious will. All things have been delivered to me by my Father; and no one knows the Son except the Father, and no one knows the Father except the Son and any one to whom the Son chooses to reveal him . . .

If I glorify myself, my glory is nothing; it is my Father who glorifies me, of whom you say that he is your God. But you have not known him; I know him. If I said, I do not know him, I should be a liar like you; but I do know him and I keep his word.

—Obedience. Life in a family is impossible unless there is a real measure of willingness on the part of the child to listen to his father and respect his wishes. It can never be a total obedience and it is for a limited period. The writer of Proverbs speaks in this way about this relationship of obedience:

My son, do not forget my teaching,
    but let your heart keep my commandments.

Hear, O sons, a father's instruction,
    and be attentive, that you may gain insight;
for I give you good precepts:
    do not forsake my teaching.
When I was a son with my father,

tender, the only one in the sight of my mother, he taught me . . .

When applied to Jesus the idea of sonship points to his complete obedience to God the Father. This submission springs out of love:

The Son can do nothing of his own accord, but only what he sees the Father doing; for whatever he does, that the Son does likewise. For the Father loves the Son, and shows him all that he himself is doing.

Weren't there many myths about gods coming to earth and about virgin births? And what is the difference between the incarnation of Jesus and the incarnations of Hindu gods?

Is there really anything unique about the belief that Jesus is a God-man? Was it not a common idea at the time? Is it not obvious that the early Christians took over the idea from pagan sources around them?

▷ The background to the stories of gods coming to earth is always polytheistic. They arise out of the belief that there are many gods with different functions and powers, and with a special interest in particular people or places. This is very different from the biblical idea of the one Creator-God who is 'the Lord of all the earth'. In Hinduism, the concept of 'God' as the 'universal Spirit' is very different from the Christian understanding of the infinite, personal God. (See BOOK TWO, pp. 25 and 11 ff.).

▷ Many of the ancient myths about gods coming to earth were associated with the mystery religions or the fertility cults, whose rituals were intended to assist the annual cycle of nature. (See further pp. 108f.).

Thomas Boslooper concludes a comparative study of such stories by underlining the vast difference in outlook between the biblical account and the other stories:

The story of the virgin birth is as different from pagan 'analogies' as monotheism is from polytheism, as different as biblical ideas of the relationship between God and man are from the mythological activities of gods in human affairs, and as different as the polygamous and incestuous pagan society was from the Christian teaching on morals and marriage. Primitive Christianity as opposed to Gentile thought (Greek, Roman, Egyptian, Babylonian and Persian) believed in marriage as over against asceticism and monogamy as over against

polygamy. Over against early Catholic Christianity (as reflected in apocryphal tradition) and Buddhist thought, it believed that sex in itself was not sinful and that moral order could result from the human process of birth. Furthermore, primitive Christianity did not project its hope for a new society into the life of the gods, i.e. into suprahuman speculation. Its hope for humanity lay in reflection on him who was the first in a new order within society.

Professor Zaehner, who himself writes out of a Hindu background, emphasizes the vast difference between Christian assumptions and Hindu assumptions. The incarnation of Jesus, therefore, has little or no connection with Hindu incarnations of 'God'.

. . . to maintain that all religions are paths leading to the same goal, as is frequently done today, is to maintain something that is not true.

Not only on the dogmatic, but also on the mystical plane, too, there is no agreement.

It is then only too true that the basic principles of Eastern and Western, which in practice means Indian and Semitic, thought are, I will not say irreconcilably opposed; they are simply not starting from the same premises. The only common ground is that the function of religion is to provide release; there is no agreement at all as to what it is that man must be released from. The great religions are talking at cross purposes.

It is therefore foolish to discuss either Hinduism or Buddhism in Christian terms; and it is at least as foolish to try to bring the New Testament into harmony with the Vedanta. They do not deal with the same subject matter. Even Indian theism is not comparable with Christianity in a way that, for example, Zoroastrianism and Islam are; nor are the various avatars of Vishnu really comparable to the Christian doctrine of the Incarnation.

QUESTION SIX

"What is the meaning of the death of Jesus?"

Does the death of Jesus mean anything more than the death of any other historical figure? Did it achieve anything?

Our answers to these questions will depend partly on our general assumptions about Jesus, and partly on our interpretation of the Old Testament and the Gospel accounts.

THE OLD TESTAMENT BACKGROUND

The teaching of the Old Testament formed the background of the thinking of Jesus and the disciples. The following are some of the basic truths which they would have learned from the Old Testament.

The relationship between God and man

The Old Testament speaks of both the *personal* aspect and the *legal* aspect of the relationship between God and man. God deals with men in a fully personal way; but at the same time he is the one who has given man the law and who judges man by that law.

▷ *The personal aspect.* Many of the writers of the Bible describe the relationship between God and man in incredibly personal and human terms.

Hosea the prophet speaking on behalf of God:

When Israel was a child, I loved him . . .
The more I called them,
  the more they went from me;
they kept sacrificing to the Baals,
  and burning incense to idols.

Yet it was I who taught Ephraim to walk,
  I took them up in my arms;
  but they did not know that I healed them.
I led them with the chords of compassion,
  with the bands of love,
and I became to them as one
  who eases the yoke from their jaws,
  and I bent down to them and fed them.

▷ *The legal aspect.* This is how Moses speaks about the laws which God has given to the nation:

All the commandments which I command you this day you shall be careful to do, that you may live and multiply, and go in and possess the land which the Lord swore to give to your fathers . . . So you shall keep the commandments of the Lord your God, by walking in his ways and by fearing him . . . Take heed lest you forget the Lord your God, by not keeping his commandments and his ordinances and his statutes, which I command you this day . . . And if you forget the Lord your God and go after other gods and serve them and worship them, I solemnly warn you this day that you shall surely perish. Like the nations that the Lord makes to perish before you, so shall you perish, because you would not obey the voice of the Lord your God.

God's attitude to man the sinner

God is both loving and holy. This means that he loves the sinner and longs for the very best for him; but at the same time he cannot accept man's rebellion lightly. He is not morally neutral, and he cannot simply forgive the sin of those who persist in their rebellion against him and refuse to accept their guilt before him. He cannot turn a blind eye or act as if nothing had happened. Man's sin is a personal affront to God; but it is also at the same time a violation of his laws. And when the laws are broken, the sanctions must be applied. Thus God's reaction to man in his sin can be summed up in two words: love and wrath.

This is what God reveals to *Moses* about his own character:

The Lord, the Lord, a God merciful and gracious, slow to anger, and abounding in steadfast love and faithfulness, keeping steadfast love for thousands, forgiving iniquity and transgression and sin, but who will by no means clear the guilty . . .

These are the words of *Jeremiah* speaking on behalf of God:

How can I pardon you?
  Your children have forsaken me,
  and have sworn by those who are no gods.
When I fed them to the full,
  they committed adultery
  and trooped to the houses of harlots.
They were well-fed lusty stallions,
  each neighing for his neighbour's wife.
Shall I not punish them for these things?
  says the Lord.

These are the words of *Ezekiel* speaking on behalf of God:

Have I any pleasure in the death of the wicked, says the Lord God, and not rather that he should turn from his way and live?

The connection between sin and death

The book of Genesis speaks of death as an intruder in the human race, and as something which is closely tied up with man's rebellion against God. It tells how God tested the obedience of Adam and Eve:

The Lord God commanded the man, saying, 'You may freely eat of every tree of the garden; but of the tree of the knowledge of good and evil you shall not eat, for in the day that you eat of it you shall die.'

Adam and Eve chose to disobey because they wanted to become gods themselves and to cease being dependent on their Creator. And these were some of the consequences of their disobedience:

more acute physical suffering;

physical death (although we are not told what human life would have been like if they had not been disobedient);

they forfeited the possibility of living in constant fellowship and communion with God.

This Old Testament teaching about the inseparable connection between sin and death is summarized by *Paul* and *James* in these words:

Sin came into the world through one man and death through sin, and so death spread to all men because all men sinned.

The wages of sin is death . . .

. . . desire when it has conceived gives birth to sin; and sin when it is full-grown brings forth death.

Dealing with sin and its consequences

The sacrificial system points to a way of 'bearing sin'. The New Testament writers were familiar with all the sacrifices of the Old Testament period. And they regarded them as part of a system instituted by God himself to teach fundamental truths about his dealings with men.

▷ The expression 'to bear sin (or sins)' means 'to be responsible for sin and to bear the consequences of it.'
  For instance, when a person breaks the laws of God governing social life and worship,

---

Top: *In India a worshipper touches the arm of a priest to identify himself with the offering to the gods. The priest is the official go-between.*

Bottom left: *Present-day Samaritans celebrate the Feast of the Passover on Mount Gerizim. Twelve sheep are slaughtered over a sunken stone altar.*

Bottom right: *The Moslem pilgrim to Mecca still offers a blood sacrifice – usually a sheep, but occasionally cattle or even camels. The animals are bought from traders at up to twice their market value.*

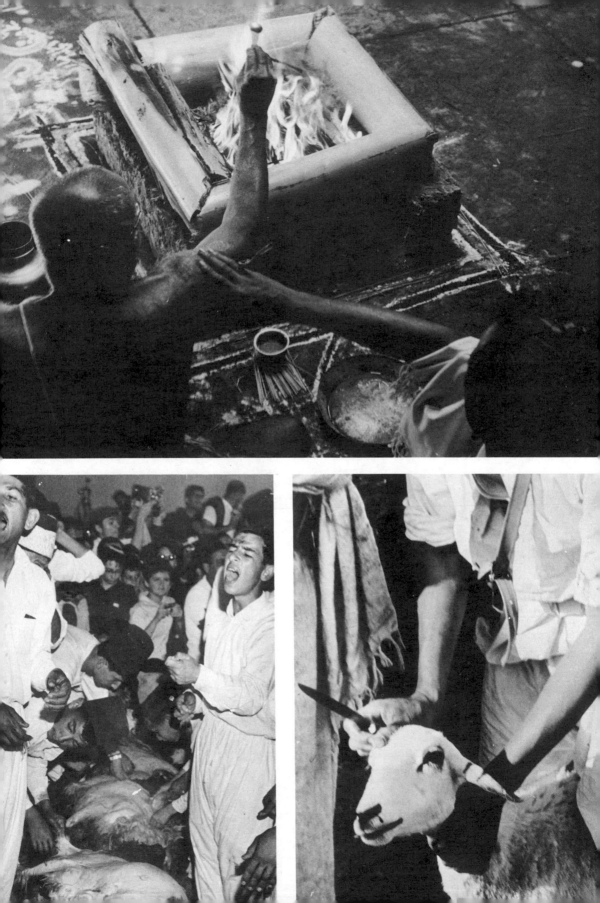

it is said of him:

> He shall *bear his iniquity.*

> He shall *bear his sin.*

This amounts to saying, 'He shall be responsible for the wrong he has done; and he shall bear the punishment which his wrongdoing deserves.'

▷ In one case we read that one person can bear the sins of another person:

He shall *bear her iniquity.*

In the sacrificial system certain animals are said to 'bear sin':

The sin offering . . . has been given to you (the sons of Aaron, the priests) that you may *bear the iniquity* of the congregation.

▷ On the Day of Atonement each year Aaron was to confess the sins of the people as he laid his hands on the head of the goat, and . . .

the goat shall *bear all their iniquities* upon him to a solitary land.

These sacrifices were intended to bring home to the Jew in a vivid and dramatic way certain basic truths:

> that sin and guilt have to be punished;

> that if men bear the consequences of their sin and guilt, it means death;

> that forgiveness is available to men, not because God turns a blind eye to sin and acts as if it does not exist, but because the full responsibility and consequences of it can be borne by another;

> that the sacrifices were not simply the expression of homage of man the creature to his Creator, but also of man the sinner to the God against whom he had sinned;

> that there is a way by which the guilty party can be acquitted and forgiven without setting aside or annulling the law of God.

▷ The prophet *Isaiah* speaks not of an animal bearing sin, but of *a person* who will bear sins. He is speaking about someone whom he calls 'the Servant of the Lord', and

A Roman execution. To the Jews the man who was hanged died under God's curse. Crucifixion of the Messiah was therefore unthinkable.

these are some of the things which he says about him:

He was wounded for our transgressions,
 he was bruised for our iniquities;
upon him was the chastisement that made us whole,
 and with his stripes we are healed . . .
The Lord has laid on him the iniquity of us all.

He shall *bear their iniquities.*

He *bore the sin* of many.

Yet it was the will of the Lord to bruise him;
 he has put him to grief;

when he makes himself an offering for sin,
    he shall see his offspring, he shall prolong
    his days.

The identity of the Servant of the Lord is left open. Isaiah can hardly be speaking of himself or of any known person or of the nation as a whole when he speaks about him 'bearing sins'.

The death penalty

Under the Old Testament law *the death penalty* was prescribed for various offences:

Whoever curses his God shall bear his sin. He who blasphemes the name of the Lord shall be put to death.

A hanged person was regarded as being *under a curse from God:*

If a man has committed a crime punishable by death and he is put to death, and you hang him on a tree, his body shall not remain all night upon the tree; but you shall bury him the same day, for a hanged man is accursed by God.

JESUS' OWN TEACHING ABOUT HIS DEATH

Mark records three predictions which Jesus made of his approaching death:

And he began to teach them that the Son of man must suffer many things, and be rejected by the elders and the chief priests and the scribes, and be killed, and after three days rise again. And he said this plainly.

They went on from there and passed through Galilee. And he would not have any one know it; for he was teaching his disciples, saying to them, 'The Son of man will be delivered into the hands of men, and they will kill him; and when he is killed, after three days he will rise.'

And they were on the road, going up to Jerusalem, and Jesus was walking ahead of them; and they were amazed, and those who followed were afraid. And taking the twelve again, he began to tell them what was to happen to him, saying, 'Behold, we are going up to Jerusalem; and the Son of man will be delivered to the chief priests and the scribes, and they will condemn him to death, and deliver him to the Gentiles; and they will mock him, and spit upon him, and scourge him, and kill him; and after three days he will rise.

Jesus did not give a detailed explanation

of why he was going to die. But he gave certain important indications or clues as to what it would mean.

Jesus as the suffering Servant

Jesus identified himself with the suffering Servant of Isaiah. In his predictions of his sufferings there are echoes of the description of the suffering of the Servant. Compare, for example, Mark 8: 31, 'The Son of man must suffer many things, and be rejected . . . and be killed . . .' with Isaiah 53: 3, 8, 'He was despised and rejected by men. . . . By oppression and judgement he was taken away. . . .' And Mark 10: 15, 'The Son of man . . . came not to be served but to serve, and to give his life as a ransom for many' with Isaiah 53: 10, 'It was the will of the Lord to bruise him . . . he makes himself an offering for sin' ('ransom' is another possible translation for 'offering for sin' here).

Good news

Jesus saw his death as part of the good news which would be spread throughout the world. At a party in Bethany a short time before his death a woman anointed Jesus with expensive ointment, and there were complaints about the waste:

But Jesus said, 'Let her alone; why do you trouble her? She has done a beautiful thing to me . . . She has done what she could; she has anointed my body beforehand for burying. And truly, I say to you, wherever the gospel is preached in the whole world, what she has done will be told in memory of her.'

Connection with the Passover

Jesus connected the meaning of his death with the Passover. When he celebrated the Passover with his disciples, just before his arrest—commemorating the deliverance of Israel from Egypt—he gave some parts of the meal a new significance:

And as they were eating, he took bread, and blessed, and broke it, and gave it to them, and said, 'Take; this is my body.' And he took a cup, and when he had given thanks he gave it to them, and they all drank of it. And he said to them, 'This is my blood of the covenant, which is poured out for many. Truly, I say to you, I shall not drink again of the fruit of the vine until that day when I drink it new in the kingdom of God.'

God's judgement on sin

Jesus connected his death with the judgement of God on human sin. He thought of the suffering and death before him as 'a cup' held out to him by the Father:

And going a little farther he fell on his face and prayed, 'My Father, if it be possible, let this cup pass from me; nevertheless, not as I will, but as thou wilt.'

Again, for the second time, he went away and prayed, 'My Father, if this cannot pass unless I drink it, thy will be done.'

There is an echo here of the many passages in the Old Testament which speak of the cup of the wrath of God—for example:

For in the hand of the Lord there is a cup,
    with foaming wine, well mixed;
and he will pour a draught from it,
    and all the wicked of the earth
    shall drain it down to the dregs.

Thus the Lord, the God of Israel, said to me: 'Take from my hand this cup of the wine of wrath, and make all the nations to whom I send you drink it. They shall drink and stagger and be crazed because of the sword which I am sending among them.

Rouse yourself, rouse yourself,
    stand up, O Jerusalem,
you who have drunk at the hand of the Lord
    the cup of his wrath,
who have drunk to the dregs
    the bowl of staggering.

THE CIRCUMSTANCES OF HIS DEATH

Jesus' last week is reported in all four Gospels in much greater detail than any other period of his life; and this suggests that the writers saw a great deal of significance in the actual events which led up to his death. If we put the four accounts together, certain points stand out very clearly.

▷ He went to his death voluntarily. The words and actions of Jesus provoked opposition from the religious authorities at a very early stage in his ministry. And when Jesus made his final journey to Jerusalem he knew that he was going to die.

He must have known what was involved in scourging and execution at the hands of the Romans. They would use a flagellum, a whip of leather thongs, to which small pieces of metal or bone were tied. People sometimes died under the scourge. The procedure for crucifixion was this: the two hands were nailed to the cross-beam while the victim was still on the ground; the cross-beam would then be drawn up by ropes and fastened to the upright part of the cross. The feet would then be nailed to the upright. The victim rarely died in less than 36 hours, but could be put out of his misery at any time by having his legs broken with a hammer, which would soon lead to suffocation; or his side could be pierced by a sword.

Right up to the moment before his arrest, Jesus was aware that he could avoid this kind of death if he wanted to. He did not believe that he was caught in a trap from which he could not escape.

They went to a place which was called Gethsemane . . . And he took with him Peter and James and John, and began to be greatly distressed and troubled. And he said to them, 'My soul is very sorrowful, even to death . . .' And going a little farther, he fell on the ground and prayed that, if it were possible, the hour might pass from him. And he said, 'Abba, Father, all things are possible to thee; remove this cup from me; yet not what I will, but what thou wilt.'

▷ It is significant also that he had done nothing to deserve the death penalty. The Jewish authorities realized that their own charge of blasphemy would mean nothing according to Roman law. They therefore handed him over to Pilate, the Roman Governor, on a charge of treason against the state. They accused him of claiming to be 'the king of the Jews' and thereby posing a threat to the authority of Caesar:

And Pilate asked him, 'Are you the King of the Jews?' And he answered him, 'You have said so.' . . . Pilate again said to them, 'Then what shall I do with the man you call the King of the Jews?' And they cried out again, 'Crucify him.' And Pilate said to them, 'Why, what evil has he done?' But they shouted all the more, 'Crucify him.' So Pilate, wishing to satisfy the crowd, released for them Barabbas; and having scourged Jesus, he delivered him to be crucified.

Pilate tried in three ways to avoid passing

the sentence of death which the Jewish authorities wanted him to pass:

> he tried to pass the responsibility over to Herod, the puppet king;

> he offered to punish Jesus simply with a flogging and then to release him;

> and finally he offered to release Jesus as a gesture of goodwill during the Passover feast.

But the Jewish authorities and the crowd were not satisfied, and in the end Pilate passed the sentence of death on Jesus simply to satisfy their demands and avoid a riot.

It was obvious to at least four people that he had done nothing to deserve the death penalty:

Pilate:

I find no crime in him.

Herod:

Nothing deserving death has been done by him.

One of the criminals crucified with Jesus:

We are receiving the due reward of our deeds; but this man has done nothing wrong.

The *Roman centurion* who watched him dying:

Certainly this man was innocent!

Jesus' last recorded words

And when they came to the place which is called The Skull, there they crucified him, and the criminals, one on the right and one on the left. And Jesus said, 'Father forgive them; for they know not what they do.

When Jesus saw his mother, and the disciple whom he loved standing near, he said to his mother, 'Woman behold your son!' Then he said to the disciple, 'Behold your mother!'

One of the criminals being crucified beside Jesus began mocking him, but later came to change his mind about him:

And he said, 'Jesus, remember me when you come in your kingly power.' And he said to him, 'Truly, I say to you, today you will be with me in Paradise.'

At the ninth hour Jesus cried with a loud voice, 'Eloi, Eloi, lama sabachthani?' which means, 'My God, my God, why hast thou forsaken me?'

Then Jesus, crying with a loud voice, said, 'Father, into thy hands I commit my spirit!'

After this Jesus, knowing that all was now finished, said (to fulfil the scripture), 'I thirst.' A bowl full of vinegar stood there; so they put a sponge full of the vinegar on hyssop and held it to his mouth. When Jesus had received the vinegar, he said, 'It is finished'; and he bowed his head and gave up his spirit.

The 'Pavement' of the Roman Fort of Antonia where Jesus was tried was discovered earlier this century. These stones are scratched with games the soldiers played.

What is the meaning of the death of Jesus?

"He died as an example—
his death shows us
something about God
and man" PAGE 63

"His death has no
special meaning"
PAGE 66

"His death achieved
something—he was
bearing our sins"
PAGE 57

"The cross is merely
a symbol—any inter-
pretation is 'myth'"
PAGE 68

ANSWER 1: BIBLICAL CHRISTIANITY

"His death achieved something—he was bearing our sins"

This is to say, Jesus was bearing the guilt and consequences of human sin. He was dying in our place and enduring what we deserve for our proud rebellion against our Creator. His death can deal with the guilt of our past, and can bring us into a new relationship with God in the present. We can enjoy increasing deliverance from the power of sin in our lives and all the other positive benefits of his death.

Almost every writer of the New Testament gives an explanation of *how* the death of Jesus achieved something. They take as their starting-point that the death of Jesus deals with the sin of men:

John records John the Baptist's description of Jesus:

Behold, the Lamb of God, who *takes away* (i.e. bears) *the sin* of the world.

. . . Jesus Christ the righteous; and he is the *expiation for our sins*, and not for ours only but also for the sins of the whole world.

Luke records some of the last words of Jesus before his ascension:

Thus it is written, that the Christ should suffer and on the third day rise from the dead, and that repentance and *forgiveness of sins* should be preached in his name to all nations . . .

Peter:

He himself *bore our sins* in his body on the tree.

Christ . . . *died for sins* once for all, the righteous for the unrighteous, that he might bring us to God.

Paul:

Christ died *for our sins*.

The writer to the Hebrews:

. . . he . . . *made purification for sins* . . .

POINTS TO CONSIDER ABOUT THIS ANSWER

This answer makes sense of the Old Testament background.

▷ It takes seriously both the *personal* aspect of the relationship between God and man, and also the *legal* aspect. There is through the cross, both forgiveness for the personal injury to God and for the disobedience to his laws:

And you, who were dead in trespasses and the uncircumcision of your flesh, God made alive together with him, having forgiven us all our trespasses, having cancelled the bond which stood against us with its legal demands; this he set aside, nailing it to the cross.

▷ It does justice both to the *wrath* of God and to the *love* of God towards the sinner.

It is the love of God which turns aside the wrath of God and all its consequences:

God shows his love for us in that while we were yet sinners Christ died for us. Since, therefore, we are now justified by his blood, much more shall we be saved by him from the wrath of God.

In this is love, not that we loved God but that he loved us and sent his Son to be the propitiation for our sins.

The word propitiation conveys the idea of turning aside the wrath of God.

▷ It fits in with the close connection which the Old Testament sees between *sin* and *death*.

The death he died he died to sin, once for all, but the life he lives he lives to God.

The wages of sin is death, but the free gift of God is eternal life in Christ Jesus our Lord.

▷ It explains how the system of sacrifices, which were said to 'bear sin', has been fulfilled:

When Christ had offered for all time a single sacrifice for sins, he sat down at the right hand of God, then to wait until his enemies should be made a stool for his feet. For by a single offering he has perfected for all time those who are sanctified. . . . Where there is forgiveness . . . , there is no longer any offering for sin.

▷ It explains the sense in which Jesus could be under a *curse* from God as he hung on the cross:

Christ redeemed us from the curse of the law, having become a curse for us—for it is written, 'Cursed be every one who hangs on a tree' . . .

It makes sense of Jesus' own teaching about his death.

▷ It explains why he identified himself with the Servant of the Lord in the book of Isaiah.

Thus, when *Peter* writes about the meaning of the death of Jesus there are very definite echoes of the passages about the Servant who bears sins:

He committed no sin; no guile was found on his lips (1 Peter 2:22) / He had done no violence, and there was no deceit in his mouth (Isaiah 53:9)

He was reviled (1 Peter 2: 23) / He was despised and rejected by men (Isaiah 53: 3)

He himself bore our sins (1 Peter 2: 24) / He bore the sin of many (Isaiah 53: 12)

By his wounds you have been healed (1 Peter 2: 24) / With his stripes we are healed (Isaiah 53: 5)

You were straying like sheep (1 Peter 2: 25) / All we like sheep have gone astray (Isaiah 53: 6)

▷ It explains how he could think of his death as being part of the good news for all men. For if his death is connected with God's forgiveness, then his death is part of the good news which must be spread to all men.

Thus, *Jesus* explains to the disciples after his resurrection:

Then he opened their minds to understand the scriptures, and said to them, 'Thus it is written, that the Christ should suffer and on the third day rise from the dead, and that repentance and forgiveness of sins should be preached in his name to all nations, beginning from Jerusalem. . .'

▷ It explains why he connected his death with the Passover. We can begin to understand the intention of Jesus when we notice the significance of the first Passover. On the night before the Israelites' deliverance from Egypt, each household killed a lamb and sprinkled some of the blood on the two doorposts and on the lintel. The flesh was cooked and eaten with bread and herbs. This was the meaning of the ceremony:

It is the Lord's passover. For I will pass through the land of Egypt that night, and I will smite all the first-born in the land of Egypt, both man and beast . . . The blood shall be a sign for you, upon the houses where you are; and when I see the blood, I will pass over you, and no plague shall fall upon you to destroy you, when I smite the land of Egypt.

This is how the children of Israel were commanded to commemorate each year the deliverance from Egypt:

Observe the month of Abib, and keep the passover to the Lord your God; for in the month of Abib the Lord your God brought you out of Egypt by night. And you shall offer the passover sacrifice to the Lord your God, from the flock or the herd . . . seven days you shall eat it with unleavened bread, the bread of affliction . . . that all the days of your life you may remember the day when you came out of the land of Egypt.

Jesus' death achieved a new deliverance for men. Thus *Paul* writes:

Christ, our paschal lamb, has been sacrificed.

Peter:

You know that you were ransomed from the futile ways inherited from your fathers, not with perishable things such as silver or gold, but with the precious blood of Christ, like that of a lamb without blemish or spot.

▷ It explains how he connected his death with the judgement of God on human sin. If Jesus bore our sins, he has also borne the condemnation that we deserve.

Thus *Paul* writes:

There is therefore now no condemnation for those who are in Christ Jesus. For the law of the Spirit of life in Christ Jesus has set me free from the law of sin and death. For God has done what the law, weakened by the flesh, could not do: sending his own Son in the likeness of sinful flesh and for sin, he condemned sin in the flesh . . .

It makes sense of the circumstances of his death.

▷ It accounts for Jesus' willingness to go through suffering and death, which he could easily have avoided if he had wanted to. Thus, when Peter starts to fight to defend Jesus:

Jesus said to Peter, 'Put your sword in its sheath; shall I not drink the cup which the Father has given me?'

▷ It makes sense of some of his last words:

'Father forgive them . . .' His attitude towards those who killed him is a demonstration of the willingness of God to forgive.

One of the criminals asked Jesus to remember him when he came in his kingly power. Jesus answered 'Today you will be with me in Paradise.' He thus pointed to the victory and royal triumph which would immediately be won by his death.

'My God, my God, why hast thou forsaken me?' If we are prepared to take these words at their face value, we must recognize that Jesus was *not* saying, 'O God, I feel as if you

have forsaken me—although I trust that you must still be with me.' What he was saying, rather, was something much more profound and horrifying: 'My God, my God, *you have forsaken me. Why?*' These words begin to make sense if we understand that Jesus was in a real sense bearing the judgement of God on man's sin.

'It is finished.' These words would suggest that Jesus was conscious of something that had been achieved through all his suffering and agony. He was conscious not only that his life was ending, but also that he had accomplished something of a permanent and lasting nature.

This interpretation also makes sense of the many different metaphors which the New Testament writers used to describe what Jesus achieved by his death. It also shows how these different metaphors are related to each other, because it provides a basic link which binds them together.

▷ The metaphor of *justification* comes from the law court and means simply 'acquittal'. If Jesus was bearing the judgement of God on human sin, then for those who believe in Jesus and accept for themselves the benefits of his death, there is complete acquittal before God. The verdict of 'guilty' no longer stands against them, and they can now enjoy fellowship with God without fear or shame.

Therefore, since we are justified by faith, we have peace with God through our Lord Jesus Christ . . . God shows his love for us in that while we were yet sinners Christ died for us.

▷ The metaphor of *redemption* or *ransom* comes from the Old Testament idea of the kinsman redeemer and from the slave-market, where a person could be redeemed through the payment of a fee. This metaphor, therefore, emphasizes that the forgiveness God offers on the basis of the death of Jesus cost him something. There was no simple announcement of forgiveness. It shows that if it costs men something to forgive each other, the cost for God in forgiving rebellious man is infinitely greater.

You know that you were ransomed from the futile ways inherited from your fathers, not with perishable things such as silver or gold, but with

the precious blood of Christ . . .

▷ The metaphor of *victory* emphasizes that in the death of Jesus a decisive victory was won over sin and death and over the supernatural powers of evil which lie behind the rebellion of the human race against God. By this victory he had liberated men who were held prisoners of sin, death and the Devil. If Jesus was bearing the sins of men when he died on the cross, we have an explanation as to *why* and *how* Jesus was able to gain the victory over the Devil.

. . . You, who were dead in trespasses and the uncircumcision of your flesh, God made alive together with him, having forgiven us all our trespasses, having cancelled the bond which stood against us with its legal demands; this he set aside, nailing it to the cross. He disarmed the principalities and powers and made a public example of them, triumphing over them in him.

▷ The metaphor of *reconciliation* stresses that man has broken off relations with God, and also that God cannot turn a blind eye to man's rebellion against him and act as if nothing had happened. If we understand that Jesus was dying in our place on the cross, this metaphor stresses that God himself has taken the initiative in doing something to win men back into fellowship with himself.

God shows his love for us in that while we were yet sinners Christ died for us . . . For if while we were enemies we were reconciled to God by the death of his Son, much more, now that we are reconciled, shall we be saved by his life. Not only so, but we also rejoice in God through our Lord Jesus Christ, through whom we have now received our reconciliation.

▷ The metaphor of *salvation* comes from the many occasions in the Old Testament when the children of Israel were delivered or saved from a desperate situation. If we think of the death of Jesus as the remedy for the guilt and power of sin, then the word 'salvation' stresses the completeness of the deliverance from the consequences and the power of sin which is available through the death of Christ. If Christ was bearing sins on the cross, this is the means by which the deliverance has been achieved.

Since, therefore, we are now justified by his blood, much more shall we be saved by him from the wrath of God.

This answer provides us with a starting-point from which we can go on to see what the death of Jesus must mean in the experience of the individual Christian. To say that Jesus was bearing the sins of men when he died on the cross by no means exhausts all that can or should be said about the death of Jesus. But without this basic starting-point, anything else that we may say lacks an adequate foundation and leaves many questions unanswered.

▷ The way in which Jesus reacted to undeserved abuse and suffering is an example which the Christian is bound to follow:

Christ . . . suffered for you, leaving you an example, that you should follow in his steps. He committed no sin; no guile was found on his lips. When he was reviled, he did not revile in return; when he suffered, he did not threaten; but he trusted him who judges justly.

Left: *Samaritans prepare for the midnight Passover Feast in modern Israel. The Passover commemorates the night in Egypt when Israel's firstborn sons were saved from death.*

Right: *The Paschal lamb is tethered, ready to be killed and roasted at the Easter festival in Greece.*

. . . rejoice in so far as you share Christ's sufferings, that you may also rejoice and be glad when his glory is revealed.

▷ The way in which Jesus renounced self-interest and went to the cross for the sake of others shows the Christian that he too must say no to his self-centredness and be willing to be closely identified with Jesus in the eyes of the world. He must also be prepared to receive the same kind of treatment that Jesus received.

If any man would come after me, let him deny himself and take up his cross daily and follow me . . . For whoever is ashamed of me and of my words, of him will the Son of man be ashamed when he comes in his glory and the glory of the Father and of the holy angels.

This is how *Paul* longs to be identified fully with Jesus; he wants to receive his righteousness, to share his sufferings and be like him in his denial of self in death:

. . . whatever gain I had, I counted as loss for the sake of Christ. Indeed I count everything as loss because of the surpassing worth of knowing Christ Jesus my Lord. For his sake I have suffered the loss of all things, and count them as refuse, in order that I may gain Christ and be found in him, not having a righteousness of my own, based on law, but that which is through faith in Christ, the righteousness from God that depends on faith; that I may know him and the power of his resurrection, and may share his sufferings, becoming like him in his death. . . .

Jesus' willingness to die to self when he went to the cross is the strongest possible plea that we should die to self and live for him and not ourselves:

. . . the love of Christ controls us, because we are convinced that one has died for all; therefore all have died. And he died for all, that those who live might live no longer for themselves but for him who for their sake died and was raised.

The way that Jesus went willingly to death, the death of the worst kind of criminal, is a powerful incentive to an attitude of humility:

Have this mind among yourselves, which you have in Christ Jesus, who, though he was in the form of God, did not count equality with God a thing to be grasped, but emptied himself, taking the form of a servant, being born in the likeness of men. And being found in human form he humbled himself and became obedient unto death, even death on a cross . . .

Jesus' death for all men must affect our attitude to others as we realize their value before God. We are not to despise any individual, for he is

. . . the brother for whom Christ died.

When the Christian shares the suffering of Christ, he can also experience the comfort and consolation of Christ. And this in turn can be shared with all Christ's people:

Blessed be the God and Father of our Lord Jesus Christ, the Father of all mercies and God of all comfort, who comforts us in all our affliction, so that we may be able to comfort those who are in any affliction, with the comfort with which we ourselves are comforted by God. For as we share abundantly in Christ's sufferings, so through Christ we share abundantly in comfort too. If we are afflicted, it is for your comfort and salvation; and if we are comforted, it is for your comfort, which you experience when you patiently endure the same sufferings that we suffer. Our hope for you is unshaken; for we know that as you share in our sufferings, you will also share in our comfort.

▷ Death is no longer to be feared, because it brings us into the presence of Christ. Christ's death has taken the 'sting' out of death for us.

The sting of death is sin, and the power of sin is the law. But thanks be to God, who gives us the victory through our Lord Jesus Christ.

. . . to me to live is Christ, and to die is gain.

The Christian is not afraid, if necessary, to die for his faith. John speaks of the victory of believers, who, in their own lives in the world are able to defeat Satan through the power of Jesus' death:

And I heard a loud voice in heaven, saying, 'Now the salvation and the power and the kingdom of our God and the authority of his Christ have come, for the accuser of our brethren has been thrown down, who accuses them day and night before our God. And they have conquered him by the blood of the Lamb and by the word of their testimony, for they loved not their lives even unto death. Rejoice then, O heaven and you that dwell therein! . . . '

If you give this answer about the meaning of the death of Jesus, you should go on to consider the question of the resurrection.

ANSWER 2

"He died as an example—his death shows us something about God and man"

The meaning of Christ's death is to be seen primarily in what it teaches us and in how it influences us. His death is an example of self-sacrifice, of non-resistance in the face of evil and injustice, and of patient endurance of undeserved suffering. His attitude and behaviour in facing death give a demonstration of the love of God, and give us an example to follow when we face suffering ourselves.

On this view, it is not important to ask whether Jesus actually achieved anything at the time when he died on the cross; his death achieves something only when it moves me here and now. In his life he proclaimed the willingness of God to forgive sin; and his death is simply a further demonstration of the love of God, because it shows us the lengths to which Jesus was prepared to go to win us back to God. His death is also a demonstration of the sinfulness of man, because it exposes the pride and selfishness of human nature. Evil is shown up in its true colours when it comes face to face with the holy Son of God.

The message of the death of Jesus, therefore, is this: 'This is what God is like—look how far love was prepared to go for us. And this is what human nature is like—look and see what you are by nature.' As we look at the crucified Jesus, therefore, we ought to be moved to turn to him in repentance and faith. We ought to come to God to ask for forgiveness and to put our faith in Jesus as the one who shows us that we are accepted by God.

J. W. C. Wand explains what theologians

have called the 'Exemplarist Theory' of the atonement:

This is the view that we are changed in conformity with the example of Jesus. That example is so beautiful, so overwhelming in its beauty, that it has the power to transform anyone who sincerely considers it and is prepared to yield to it. 'We needs must love the highest when we see it', and living it be changed by it.

The typical illustration of this divine alchemy is the incident of the penitent thief on Calvary. In the midst of his sufferings he had evidently been so moved by the patience and calmness of the Person who hung between him and his blaspheming fellow bandit that he attained some kind of belief in the crucified Messiah and prayed to be taken into his kingdom. The contrast between the two robbers has stirred the imagination of Christians all down the ages, and change in the penitent thief has always been taken as an indication of what the example of Christ can do.

David Edwards:

The Creator of the universe was willing to suffer everything in order that the nails which harpooned and bloodily smashed the human life in which he was expressing himself might also pin down our wandering thoughts and stab our consciences awake.

POINTS TO CONSIDER ABOUT THIS ANSWER

▷ This answer contains many important aspects of the first answer (pp.57ff.), but it leaves many important questions unanswered. For example, *how* and *why* can the death of Jesus on a criminal's cross become a demonstration of the love of God? One could make out a good case for seeing it as a demonstration not so much of the love of God, but of the cruelty or callousness or weakness of God. For how could God the Father 'stand by' and do nothing while God the Son was being tortured to death? If a man stands by and does nothing while he watches his wife being beaten to death, this does not prove his love either for his wife or for anyone else.

The problem therefore can be stated in this way: how can the death of Jesus be a demonstration of the love of God unless it actually *achieves* something? If a woman is in danger of drowning in a river and a man jumps in at considerable risk to save her, he is certainly demonstrating his concern for her. But if he fails to rescue her, the mere demonstration of his concern doesn't help her at all. The death of Jesus certainly shows the self-sacrifice, the humility and the courage of Jesus, and it may move men to pity and repentance. But how can we speak about the cross as a demonstration of the love of God if we can give no clue as to *how* or *why* it rescues men from their terrible condition?

▷ This answer has nothing to say to the person who is not in the least moved by imagining Jesus dying a cruel death on a cross. If the picture of Jesus being slowly tortured to death doesn't appeal to him or move him, he may say, 'It leaves me cold; I don't see what it has to do with me or with anyone else.' This answer could be open to the charge that it uses the death of Jesus to make a purely emotional appeal. And if this is so, the sceptic has every right to say, 'Why are you trying to pull at my heart strings in this way? Of course there is something repulsive and revolting about his death. But so what? What does it prove? Even if he is the Son of God, why should his death by itself move me to repentance any more than the deaths of other innocent people who have died even more horribly?'

▷ Whenever the New Testament writers speak of the cross as a demonstration of the love of God, they give a clue as to *why* this is so. They speak of the death of Christ as God's way of dealing with sin, and averting the consequences of sin:

God so *loved* the world that he gave his only Son, that whoever believes in him *should not perish* but have eternal life.

God is *love*. In this the love of God was made manifest among us, that God sent his only Son into the world, so that we might live through him. In this is love, not that we loved God but that he loved us and sent his Son to be *the expiation for our sins*.

God shows his *love* for us in that while we were yet sinners Christ died for us. Since, therefore, we are now justified by his blood, much more shall we be *saved by him from the wrath of God*.

Peter speaks of the example that Christians can see in the way Jesus faced suffering and death. But while he sees this as *part* of the meaning of the death of Jesus, he does not see it as the *only* meaning, or as the heart of its meaning. For in the same paragraph he goes on to speak about the death of Jesus as God's way of dealing with sin.

For what credit is it, if when you do wrong and are beaten for it you take it patiently? But if when you do right and suffer for it you take it patiently, you have God's approval. For to this you have been called, because Christ also suffered for you, leaving you an example, that you should follow in his steps. He committed no sin; no guile was found on his lips. When he was reviled, he did not revile in return; when he suffered, he did not threaten; but he trusted to him who judges justly. He himself bore our sins in his body on the tree, that we might die to sin and live to righteousness. By his wounds you have been healed . . .

▷ The root of the difficulty may well be that this answer rests on the assumption that man's basic problem is his ignorance about himself and God, and his lack of feeling towards God and Christ. What we need therefore is not someone to deal with our guilt, but rather someone to show us the truth and to melt our hard hearts. And this assumption is different in certain important respects from the biblical assumption that man's most fundamental need is for his guilt before a holy God to be dealt with. (See further BOOK TWO, Question Three, 'What is man?', pp. 53ff.)

For many, an answer like this may prove to be the starting-point for genuine Christian faith. But it is hardly adequate as a complete answer, because it leaves many questions unanswered. If you can go one step further and believe that Jesus died as a sin-bearer, then there is an adequate answer to these questions. (See pp.57ff.) And it becomes clear why the hymn-writer could say:

> Were the whole realm of nature mine,
> That were an offering far too small;
> Love so amazing, so divine,
> Demands my soul, my life, my all.

An Easter Passion play in Mexico. The emphasis is on the physical sufferings of Christ.

ANSWER 3

"His death has no special meaning"

This answer takes a number of different forms.

He died as a martyr; his death was not unique. On this view, the meaning of Christ's death is simply that it shows us how far he was prepared to go to uphold his cause. He was willing to suffer and die a cruel death rather than deny what he stood for. Just as people have died for social and political causes, so in the same way Jesus died as a martyr in his own cause. His willingness to die in this way shows how sincerely he believed in his message, and how concerned he was that others should know it.

BUT: what precisely was the cause that he died for? Did he die merely to uphold the ideal of an unselfish life or the idea of the brotherhood of man? Did he die merely to convince others that it is a good thing to love one's neighbour?

The Gospels make it clear that what the Jews objected to was not the moral teaching of Jesus, but rather his claims about himself and his relationship with God the Father. If Jesus had died merely as a martyr advocating love, it is difficult to see how the cross could ever have come to be regarded as 'good news'.

The view that Jesus died as a martyr ignores a great deal of the evidence about how Jesus thought about his death, and how his disciples came to interpret it. In the interests of truth, it is only fair to ask those who hold it to look carefully at the detailed evidence of the New Testament.

If you are not interested in discussing the details of the New Testament picture, it is likely that the real problem lies further back —in questions about God and man (BOOK TWO) or about truth (BOOK ONE).

Certain other answers which have been given by Christians come into this category, because they play down or deny the unique significance of his *death*.

It is the incarnation (i.e. the Son of God becoming man in the person of Jesus Christ), **not the death of Christ, which is the heart of the Christian message.** The mere fact that God became man and lived the kind of life he lived reveals what God is like. There was no need or necessity for Jesus to die on the cross; his incarnation and life are themselves an adequate revelation of the character of God. The way he died does not add anything to what his life achieved.

BUT: it is difficult to reconcile this answer with the teaching of the New Testament as a whole. The main centre of interest in both the Gospels and the Epistles is the crucifixion and resurrection.

This answer is sometimes based on the assumption that the material world is somehow infected with sin and needs to be redeemed. But this is contrary to the biblical view of the universe.

It is not the laying down of Christ's life in death which was the significant factor in

procuring salvation for men, but rather his offering of his risen life to the Father in heaven. We are saved in so far as we participate in his present offering of his life to the Father.

BUT: the New Testament nowhere suggests that Jesus continues to offer any sacrifice in heaven—even the sacrifice of his life. On the contrary it stresses the finality and completeness of Jesus' sacrifice.

When Christ had offered for all time a single sacrifice for sins, he sat down at the right hand of God, then to wait until his enemies should be made a stool for his feet. For by a single offering he has perfected for all time those who are sanctified.

This idea of Jesus offering his risen life to the Father is based on the assumption that in the sacrificial system of the Old Testament it was the *offering of the blood* of the animal to God that was the important thing, because the offering of the blood signified the *offering of the life* of the animal. However, the way in which the word 'blood' is used throughout the Bible would suggest rather that it signifies not so much the life that is offered to God but rather the life that is laid down in death. The offering of life cannot deal with the guilt of sin; it can only be dealt with when life is surrendered in death, which is the ultimate penalty for sin.

It was not the death of Jesus as such which saves men, but his 'repentance' on our behalf. Jesus felt our sins *as if* they were his own, and was able to repent for them on our behalf. The sympathetic or vicarious repentance of Christ and its influence on men therefore enables God to forgive men.

BUT: however sympathetically Jesus could enter into our condition, how could he repent for sins which he had not committed?

According to this view, our forgiveness and salvation are dependent on our own repentance and faith. Our repentance and faith become the *grounds* on which God forgives us. In this way we can be said to earn our salvation through repentance and faith. But the New Testament writers speak about what God has already done in the death of Jesus; and they invite us to repent and believe on these grounds. In this way our repentance and faith are our response to what God has done.

Peter writes:

You know that you were ransomed from the futile ways inherited from your fathers, not with perishable things such as silver or gold, but with the precious blood of Christ, like that of a lamb without blemish or spot . . . Through him you have confidence in God, who raised him from the dead and gave him glory, so that your faith and hope are in God.

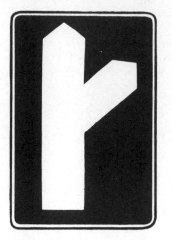

ANSWER 4

"The cross is merely a symbol— any interpretation is 'myth' "

This is to say, Jesus did not actually achieve anything when he died on the cross. We must look at the cross from our own standpoint, and see it as a symbol of what is true in human experience or what is true for us as individuals.

Rudolph Bultmann puts all the emphasis on what the cross must mean in the experience of the individual:

To believe in the cross of Christ does not mean to concern ourselves with a mythical process wrought outside of us and our world, or even an objective event turned by God to our advantage, but rather to make the cross of Christ our own, to undergo crucifixion with him. . . . The cross is not just an event of the past which can be contemplated in detachment, but the eschatological event in and beyond time, for as far as its meaning—that is, its meaning for faith—is concerned, it is an ever-present reality.

The cross and passion are ever-present realities . . . The abiding significance of the cross is that it is the judgement of the world, the judgement and the deliverance of man . . . The real meaning of the cross is that it has created a new and permanent situation in history. The preaching of the cross as the event of redemption challenges all who hear it to appropriate this significance for themselves, to be willing to be crucified with Christ.

For us the cross cannot disclose its own meaning; it is an event of the past. We can never recover it as an event in our lives.

Cross and resurrection form a single, indivisible cosmic event which brings judgement to the world and opens up for men the possibility of authentic life.

According to Bultmann, the language of the New Testament about Jesus dying for our sins is mythological language. What we must do, therefore, is to translate it into existential language which will mean something to modern man. The preaching of the cross in this way becomes a challenge to existential decision. And if we respond to the challenge in the appropriate way, we gain a deep understanding of ourselves and of the human predicament, and we can begin to enjoy authentic existence.

Colin Wilson:

The need for God I could understand, and the need for religion; I could even sympathize with the devotees like Suso or St. Francis, who weave fantasies around the Cross, the nails, and all the other traditional symbols. But ultimately I could not accept the need for redemption by a Saviour. To pin down the idea of salvation to one point in space and time seemed to me a naive kind of anthropomorphism.

Dietrich Bonhoeffer sees the cross as a symbol of 'the suffering of God in the life of the world' and of 'the participation in the powerlessness of God in the world'.

The God who makes us live in this world without using him as a working hypothesis is the God before whom we are ever standing. Before God and with him we live without God.

God allows himself to be edged out of the world and on to the cross. God is weak and powerless in the world, and that is exactly the

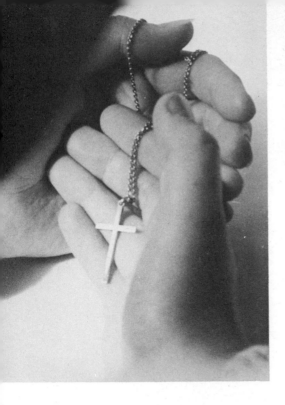

way, the only way, in which he can be with us and help us. Matthew 8: 17 makes it crystal clear that it is not by his omnipotence that Christ can help us, but by his weakness and suffering. This is the decisive difference between Christianity and all religions. Man's religiosity makes him look in his distress to the power of God in the world; he uses God as a *deus ex machina*. The Bible, however, directs him to the powerlessness and suffering of God; only a suffering God can help.

Paul van Buren interprets the death of Jesus in accordance with his understanding of existential 'freedom':

What can it mean to say, 'He *died* for our sins'? The emphasis is on his death, but we need to remember that theology, as well as the New Testament, speaks of the 'cross' or the death of Jesus as the consequence of his life. 'The cross' and other references to Jesus' death became summary ways of speaking of his whole history. as indeed his end seemed to his disciples, after the fact, to have been foreshadowed in all of his life. Since his life was one of solidarity with men, compassion for them, mercy towards their weakness and wrong, it is not surprising that his death, which was the consequence of his freedom to be related to men in this way, was spoken of as a death 'for us'. His death . . . was regarded as the measure of the freedom for which he set other men free. The man for whom the history of Jesus and his liberation of his disciples on Easter is a discernment situation of prime importance will say, 'He died for me, for my forgiveness and freedom'. When the New Testament says that he died not only for 'our' sins, 'but also for the sins of the whole world', it reflects the fact that Jesus was free for every man, those who did not acknowledge him as well as those that did, and it articulates a perspective by which all men, not just believers, are seen.

David Edwards:

The cross is the Christian symbol not only because it marked the end of the public life of Jesus of Nazareth, but also because it stands for truths of continuing experience.

As examples of these truths of experience he mentions 'inevitable suffering', 'the evil corruption of our very ideals', 'the great suffering of the innocent individual'.

Nikos Kazantzakis' novel *Christ Recrucified* describes the life of a village as it prepares to perform a Passion Play. The events of the year turn out to be a strange re-enactment of the events leading to the death of Jesus, and towards the end the Christ-figure, Manolios, is killed.

He (Pope Fotis) extended his hand and tenderly caressed the face of Manolios.
'Dear Manolios, you'll have given your life in vain,' he murmured; 'they've killed you for having taken our sins upon you; you cried: "It was I who robbed, it was I who killed and set things on fire; I, nobody else!" so that they might let the rest of us take root peacefully in these lands . . . In vain, Manolios, in vain will you have sacrificed yourself . . .'
Pope Fotis listened to the bell pealing gaily, announcing that Christ was coming down on earth to save the world . . . He shook his head and heaved a sigh: 'In vain, my Christ, in vain,' he muttered; 'two thousand years have gone by and men crucify You still. When will you be born, my Christ, and not be crucified any more, but live among us for eternity?'

Thomas Mann writes about the novel:

The novel *Christ Recrucified* is without doubt a work of high artistic order formed by a tender and firm hand and built up with strong dynamic power. I have particularly admired the poetic tact in phrasing the subtle yet unmistakable allusions to the Christian Passion story. They give the book its mythical background which is such a vital element in the epic form of today.

POINTS TO CONSIDER ABOUT THIS ANSWER

▷ This answer hardly does justice to the *whole* of the New Testament teaching. For the New Testament writers it was not a case of *either* an event which achieved something in the past *or* a truth of present experience. It was rather a case of *both/and*. The death of Jesus meant something to them in present experience because it had really achieved something for them in the first place.

▷ Is there any criterion for deciding the meaning of symbols? To some it is the very ambiguity of symbols which commends them as a means of religious communication:

F. C. Happold:

The religious symbol when examined is seen to have an ambivalent quality. It is an indefinite expression which conveys different meanings to different people. People react to religious symbols in different ways, according to their particular mental and psychological make-ups. The symbols point to something beyond themselves which is not intellectually definable, and therefore cannot be fully rationally known or described. They make perceptible what is invisible, ideal and transcendent, giving it a sort of objectivity, and so allowing it to be better apprehended.

If you treat the cross in this way, therefore, you are in effect saying, 'If the cross means something to you and something completely different to me, then it doesn't matter—because its truth is indefinable, and cannot properly be described in words. There is no such thing as "the true interpretation" of the death of Jesus; any interpretation can be true if it is true to me.' This comes very close to saying—if we may adapt the saying of Humpty Dumpty—'When I use a symbol, it means just what I choose it to mean—neither more nor less.'

This answer therefore is based on an understanding of truth which is different in certain important respects from the biblical understanding of truth. And the discussion must turn on what we mean by truth, rather than on the details of the New Testament interpretation of the death of Jesus. (See BOOK ONE, especially pp. 60ff.)

▷ Those who do not share or do not understand the basic assumptions about truth on which this answer is based, tend to react to the language of symbols with indifference or impatience:

C. E. M. Joad:

I have never been able to make anything of symbolism. A symbol I understand to be a sign for something else. Either the symbolist knows what the something else is, in which case I cannot see why he should not tell us what it is straight out, instead of obscurely hinting at it in symbols, or he does not, in which case not knowing what the symbols stand for he cannot expect his readers to find out for him. Usually, I suspect, he does not, and his symbolism is merely a device to conceal his muddled thinking.

▷ If we regard the death of Jesus on the cross as merely a symbol, we cannot at the same time claim that it is unique. Why should we not attach the same significance to the deaths of great men like Socrates or Ghandi?

▷ If salvation has not been worked out in history at a particular place and at a particular time, then the Christian message ceases to be good news about what God *has done* for man. If the saving work of Christ is extracted from history and made completely independent of history, Christian faith changes its character completely.

J. Gresham Machen outlines the alternatives in this way:

If the saving work of Christ were confined to what He does now for every Christian, there would be no such thing as a Christian gospel—an account of an event which put a new face on life. What we should have left would be simply mysticism, and mysticism is quite different from Christianity . . .

If religion be made independent of history there is no such thing as a gospel. For 'gospel' means 'good news', tidings, information about something that has happened. A gospel independent of history is a contradiction in terms.

▷ Sometimes this answer is based on assumptions about God and man which are clearly stated.

Rudolph Bultmann:

How can the guilt of one man be expiated by death of another who is sinless—if indeed we may speak of a sinless man at all? What primitive notions of guilt and righteousness does this imply? And what primitive idea of God? The rationale of sacrifice in general may of course throw some light on the theory of the atonement, but even so, what a primitive mythology it is, that a divine Being should become incarnate, and atone for the sins of men through his own blood! . . . Moreover if the Christ who died such a death was the pre-existent Son of God, what could death mean for him? Obviously very little, if he knew that he would rise again in three days!

John Robinson:

The doctrine of the Atonement is not—as in the supranaturalistic way of thinking—a highly mythological, and often rather dubious, transaction between two parties, 'God' on the one hand and 'man' on the other, who have to be brought together . . .

Even when it is Christian in content, the whole scheme of a supernatural Being coming down from heaven to 'save' mankind from sin, in the way that a man might put his finger into a glass of water to rescue a struggling insect, is frankly incredible to man 'come of age', who no longer believes in such a *deus ex machina*.

If your answer is based on assumptions of this kind about God and man, see further BOOK TWO, Question Two, 'Who or what is God?' and Question Three, 'What is man?'

BACK TO ANSWER ONE

"His death achieved something —he was bearing our sins"

PROBLEMS AND QUESTIONS

Having examined other possible answers to the basic question, we must now return to option one, the Biblical Christian answer, and look at some of the main questions and objections raised.

Is there any evidence outside the New Testament to confirm its account of the trial and death of Jesus?

The procedure of the trial of Jesus as described in the Gospels does not seem to be consistent with what we know of Jewish legal procedure of that time (for example, the fact that the trial was held at night). Is there any way of confirming whether or not the Gospels are reliable in their details?

The Jewish Encyclopedia:

Nothing corresponding to a Jewish trial took place, though it was by the action of the priests that Jesus was sent before Pontius Pilate.

▷ There are only two references to the trial of Jesus outside the New Testament, but they are so general that they hardly confirm or deny any of the details of the Gospel accounts:

Tacitus, the Roman historian (see p. 35):

. . . Christ . . . was executed in the reign of Tiberius by the Procurator Pontius Pilate . . .

The Talmud:

On the eve of Passover they hanged Yeshu of Nazareth, and the herald went before him for forty days saying, Yeshu of Nazareth is going forth to be stoned in that he hath practised sorcery and beguiled and led astray Israel. Let everyone knowing aught in his defence come and plead for him. But they found naught in his defence and hanged him on the eve of the Passover.

▷ The reliability of the Gospel writers in *other* areas, where we *can* test them, gives a fair indication as to their general reliability. For example, Luke, the writer of the Gospel and of Acts, shows an intimate knowledge of Roman law, and Acts contains accounts of Paul's encounters with Roman officials in many different places. The accurate detail of the Acts account has been confirmed at many points. If Luke's knowledge of Roman law can be relied on, it is highly likely that he took equal care to give a correct account of the events leading up to the death of Jesus. He specifically claims to have investigated all that he had heard and to have set down an ordered and accurate account.

▷ There are two possible reasons for the discrepancies between the Gospel accounts of the trial and what we know of Jewish procedure of the period.

either the Gospel writers have deliberately given a distorted and misleading account of what happened;

or the Jewish leaders were so determined to get rid of Jesus that they were prepared to break some of their own rules in order to sentence Jesus quickly and hand him over to the Romans.

Why do we need to have an 'explanation' of the death of Jesus?

Why do we need to discuss *theories* about the

meaning of the death of Jesus? Can we not

be satisfied with the *story*, and leave it to communicate its own message and make its own impact? If we insist on an explanation, aren't there a number of possible explanations, rather than just one?

▷ The New Testament writers were not satisfied with simply telling the story of what happened.

Mark records this saying of Jesus about the meaning of his death:

The Son of man . . . came . . . to give his life as a ransom for many.

Some of the events he records can only be understood as pointers to the meaning of the death of Jesus:

And Jesus uttered a loud cry, and breathed his last. And the curtain of the temple was torn in two, from top to bottom.

Peter was an eyewitness of the sufferings of Christ, and he does not hesitate to interpret the meaning of his sufferings:

Christ also died for our sins, once and for all. He, the just, suffered for the unjust, to bring us to God.

He himself bore our sins in his body on the tree.

Paul, in 1 Corinthians 15, one of the earliest passages of the New Testament, combines a statement of the bare fact of the death of Jesus ('Christ died . . .') with an interpretation of the fact ('. . . for our sins'). There is good reason to believe that he is here quoting from a summary of the gospel which he had received from the first Christians.

Therefore, if we refuse to interpret the meaning of the death of Jesus, we are being very much more agnostic than the New Testament writers.

▷ No single theory about the death of Jesus can hope to exhaust its meaning. An element of mystery will inevitably remain. But we cannot discount the meaning which Jesus and the New Testament writers clearly attached to it. Most modern hesitation about interpreting the death of Jesus starts with a reluctance or an unwillingness to accept the

clear indications that are offered in the New Testament.

▷ If we refuse to interpret the meaning of the death of Jesus, then we must allow people to interpret it in any way they wish. The Hindu, the humanist, the existentialist and the Communist will interpret it in the light of their own ways of thinking. Many of these interpretations will have little or nothing to do with the New Testament. They will often be incompatible with the New Testament and with each other. And there will be no way of deciding which interpretation is the *true* one; each one will be 'true' for the individual person. This is an approach based on a particular understanding of what truth is. (See further BOOK ONE, especially pp. 47–78.)

▷ The New Testament writers certainly speak about the death of Jesus in a great variety of ways. But if we put them all together, and compare them, is there any *basic idea* which they all have in common, and which links together the many different expressions they use? We should not be content with partial and fragmentary insights

Larry Norman, rock singer and member of the Jesus Family. He invented the slogan 'One Way' to counter the idea that all religious paths lead to God.

*The Peace Garden and Altar of Freedom in
San Francisco. Amongst a glorious profusion
of slogans, one proclaims that 'creeds divide
God's children'!*

if we can find an explanation which takes us
right to the heart of its meaning and embraces
all the different word pictures.

The answer outlined on pp. 57ff. suggests

that there *is* such a basic idea, and that it is
to be found in the idea of Jesus dying to
'bear sins'. The phrase 'bear sins' is not
simply another metaphor; it means quite
literally 'to bear the consequences of sins'.
And all the different metaphors used in the
New Testament spring from this basic idea:
that Jesus in his death dealt with human sin
by bearing its consequences and its guilt in
our place.

⚠ Why the obsession with sin ?

Lin Yutang:

What repels me particularly in religion is its
emphasis on sin. I have no consciousness of
sin and no feeling of being damned.

A. J. Ayer:

I regard the idea of original sin as morally
repulsive, and indeed am inclined to reject the
whole concept of sin as a theological survival
which can find no place in any scientific study
of human psychology.

Albert Camus:

There are words that I have never quite understood, such as sin.

▷ The Christian should be no more obsessed
with sin than a doctor is obsessed with disease.
A doctor is concerned to restore and maintain
health; and the Christian is concerned with
sin simply because he believes it to be the
basic problem of man which prevents him
from knowing God and enjoying him and his
universe. The Bible sees forgiveness of sin
not as an end in itself, but as leading to
something very positive.

Zechariah, speaking about the work of John
the Baptist, links forgiveness with the
knowledge of God:

You will go before the Lord to prepare his ways,
to give knowledge of salvation to his people
in the forgiveness of their sins . . .
(to . . . lead his people to salvation through

knowledge of him, by the forgiveness of their
sins, New English Bible).

▷ It is true that some Christians do place
an unhealthy emphasis on sin. The following
extract from the biography of D. L. Moody,
the famous nineteenth-century American
evangelist, shows how he was brought to
abandon a wrong emphasis on sin and the
wrath of God through hearing the preaching
of a young Englishman called Harry Moorhouse:

Moorhouse announced his text: 'John 3: 16:
God so loved the world, that he gave his only
begotten Son, that whosoever believeth in him
should not perish but have everlasting life.'
Instead of dividing the text into firstly, secondly,
thirdly in ministerial manner, Moody noted,
'he went from Genesis to Revelation giving proof
that God loves the sinner, and before he got
through, two or three of my sermons were
spoiled'. Moody's teaching that it was the sinner
God hates, the sinner as well as the sin, lay
shattered at his feet. 'I never knew up to that
time that God loved us so much. This heart of
mine began to thaw out; I could not keep back
my tears.'
    Moody turned in his ways, to become from
that time forth an apostle of the love of God . . .

▷ Our understanding of the word 'sin'
depends entirely on our own idea of God.
The concept is bound to be meaningless if
there is no awareness of the *God* against
whom we have sinned. (See further BOOK
TWO, Question Two 'Who or what is God?')

⚠ How can God be a God of love and a God of law at the same time ?

Behind this question lies the belief that love
and law are incompatible. If God is a God

of love he cannot at the same time be a
lawgiver and judge. If God deals with men

in a personal way, there cannot be any element of legalism in the relationship.

Kenneth Barnes:

You cannot have it both ways. Either God is a law-maker or he is the *fons et origo* of tenderness, mutuality, involvement, responsibility. For me God is in no sense a law-maker. Laws and morals are made by human beings . . . .

This objection is based on an unrealistic understanding of human love. Far from being incompatible with love, law can sometimes be an expression of it.

In the family, for example, a father makes certain rules for his children and expects them to be kept. There is no inconsistency between law and love in this case. It is the father's love for his children which makes him set certain standards for them.

Similarly, the love a husband and wife have for each other will lead them to agree certain points, simply because there are some things they will not want to do to one another. To reach an understanding of this kind is in a sense to agree about certain rules. And such an agreement is not incompatible with love; it is itself an expression of love. For love demands that they should together recognize certain limits.

If, therefore, we can say that law and love are not necessarily incompatible in personal relationships between human beings in the family, there is no reason why they should be incompatible in the relationship between God and man. The Bible refuses to drive a wedge between law and love; for the love of God towards men is a holy love. It seeks the very best for man and must set certain standards.

⚠ Why can't God forgive us as easily as we forgive one another?

If we can forgive other people when they apologize for the wrong they have done, why isn't it enough for us to repent and say to God, 'I'm sorry for the wrong I've done. Please forgive me.'

▷ In the first place, it isn't always that simple to forgive other people. If someone hurts you in a small way and apologizes, it is easy to accept the apology. But the greater the wrong or the injury, the harder it is to forgive. If a husband is unfaithful to his wife but comes back and asks forgiveness, she may be willing to forgive; but the forgiveness will not be an easy or casual thing. It will cost a great deal. It will hurt. For the essence of forgiveness is that you accept the wrong or the injury that has been done to you; you bear the consequences of it without retaliation and without being bitter or resentful.

▷ There are some circumstances in which a person can *not*, or should not, simply forgive another person, however much he may want to.

For example, a father makes certain rules for his children and expects them to be kept. If they are broken, for the child's own good there must be some kind of punishment. The father may dislike punishing his children,

and his natural instinct may be to let them off every time. But if he refuses to punish in any way, and lets the children off every time they break the rules, they are not likely to take the rules (or their father) very seriously. The end result of this indulgence is likely to be a weakening rather than a strengthening of character.

A judge in a court of law is there to administer the laws of the society. If someone has broken the laws certain sanctions must be applied. The judge may lighten the sentence; but he cannot simply forgive the offender and treat him as if the law does not exist. If this is true in human society, it is also true of the relations between God and man. If we have broken God's law, we should not imagine that we can be forgiven lightly. If the laws mean anything at all, the sanctions must be applied.

▷ If God is the Creator to whom we owe our existence, we can hardly expect him to treat us in exactly the same way as we treat our fellow creatures. The Creator-creature relationship is bound to be different in some respects from the creature-creature relationship. For example, God is himself the source and standard of what is right and good; and he has given us the law. I and my neighbour are creatures subject to the law of God, and when I wrong God, I am wronging the one whose character is utterly holy. But when I wrong my neighbour, I am wronging a fellow creature who is also a sinner.

The need for mediation or atonement arises, therefore, because man's sin—his infringement of God's laws and standards—is more serious than the injury done to a human being. It is injury to God, and a breach of his laws. It is this which makes it more difficult and costly for God to forgive man than for human beings to forgive one another.

From man's side the problem is: how can I get right with God? If I have affronted him and broken his laws, how can I make my peace with him? How can the relationship be restored?

From God's side (if we may speak in these terms) the problem is: how to uphold the laws (which God must do if he is not to deny his nature—light cannot abide darkness) and at the same time acquit the sinner. How can God forgive *and* remain just? How can he forgive (as he longs to do) and at the same time register his hatred and condemnation of everything that spoils his universe?

This is the dilemma which Paul is thinking of in Romans 3: 26 where he speaks about the cross:

. . . it was to prove at the present time that he himself is righteous and that he justifies him who has faith in Jesus . . .

B. B. Warfield sums up the problem and the need for atonement in this way:

It is the distinguishing characteristic of Christianity . . . not that it preaches a God of love, but that it preaches a God of conscience. A benevolent God, yes: men have framed a benevolent God for themselves. But a thoroughly honest God, perhaps never. That has been left for the revelation of God himself to give us. And this is the really distinguishing characteristic of the God of revelation: he is a thoroughly honest, a thoroughly conscientious God—a God who deals honestly with himself and us, who deals conscientiously with himself and with us. And a thoroughly conscientious God, we may be sure, is not a God who can deal with sinners as if they were not sinners. In this fact lies the deepest ground of the necessity of the Atonement.

⚠ The old concept of punishment is out of favour today. How can we accept an explanation which relies in any way on this theory?

People generally no longer believe in the idea of punishment as a penalty which the offender *deserves* for what he has done. Can we seriously consider an interpretation of the death of Jesus which makes use of this discredited idea?

▷ There are three basic theories of punishment:

that it is retributive: i.e. that certain crimes deserve certain punishments. If a person does *x*, then he deserves *y*. The punishment may help to reform the offender or to deter others from committing similar crimes; but these results should be considered as secondary, and as following from the fact that the punishment fits the crime.

that it is a deterrent: i.e. that any punishment is intended to deter others from doing the same thing.

that it is remedial: i.e. that any punishment or penalty is intended to benefit the offender and to enable him to change his ways.

In the past the first of these theories has generally been regarded as the most imporant of the three. Today, however, it is very widely rejected, and all the emphasis is put on the other two. Punishment is not regarded as retributive, because the idea of retribution is too close to legalized revenge; and revenge is aways wrong, whether it is taken by an individual or by the state. Thus punishment comes to be thought of basically as a way of reforming the criminal and protecting society.

What is the reason for this widespread rejection of the idea of retribution? It arises from a genuine concern for the well-being of the offender, and from revulsion against the way in which laws have often been applied in the past. But it usually goes much deeper than this, and is often based on assumptions such as these:

that there is no God, and no absolute moral standards;

that even if there is a God, moral standards have little or nothing to do with him; laws are simply social agreements arrived at by popular consensus.

These assumptions are discussed in BOOK TWO, Question Three, 'What is man?' especially pp. 75ff.

▷ There are certain serious weaknesses in the other two theories, if it is claimed that they exclude the idea of retributive punishment.

If punishment is basically a *deterrent*, what justification is there for punishment in cases where the punishment does *not* seem to deter? In these cases, punishment loses all justification and becomes arbitrary.

If, however, punishment is considered as retributive, it is something which the offender deserves for what he has done. And the unpleasantness of the suffering may well have the effect of discouraging others from committing the same offences. But the deterrent effect is in a sense a by-product; for it springs from the way in which the punishment fits the crime.

If punishment is basically *remedial*, what grounds are there for punishing a person who seems incapable of being reformed or unwilling to be reformed? As soon as it becomes evident that the offender is incapable of responding, or is deliberately refusing to respond, then the punishment becomes something arbitrary, or else it must be abandoned altogether. Sooner or later we arrive at the situation in which the offender is at the mercy of those who wish to reform him—the policeman, the judge or the psychiatrist.

If, on the other hand, punishment is basically retributive, the offender is aware that if he does *x* he will receive *y*. He therefore knows where he stands, and the law can even act as a kind of safeguard, protecting him from the whims of those who think they know what is good for him. And when the sentence

Scene from A Clockwork Orange, *in which Alex undergoes medical 'treatment' for his anti-social behaviour.*

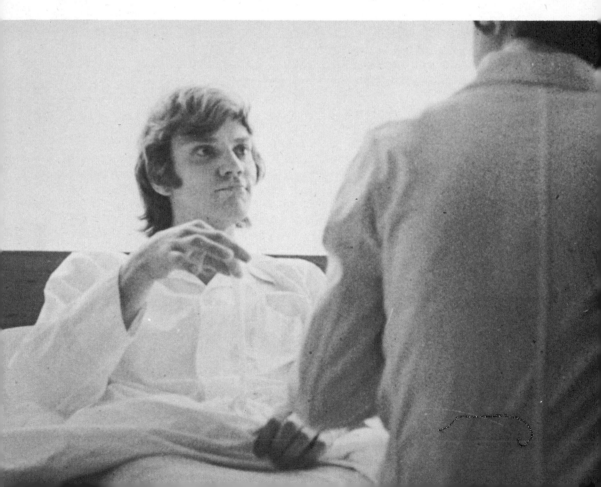

has been paid, the offender is entitled to a fresh start.

▷ The idea that we deserve to be punished for wrong-doing is basic to the teaching of the whole Bible.

At the beginning of the Bible we find that God says to Adam:

You may freely eat of every tree of the garden; but of the tree of the knowledge of good and evil you shall not eat, for in the day that you eat of it you shall die.

There is no suggestion here that physical death would come in order to reform Adam if he was disobedient, or to deter him from further sin. Death would simply be what he *deserved* for his disobedience to his Creator.

The form in which all the laws are given in the Old Testament suggests that for each crime or offence there is an appropriate—a just— penalty:

Whoever strikes his father or his mother shall be put to death.
Whoever steals a man, whether he sells him or is found in possession of him, shall be put to death.

When men strive together, and hurt a woman with child, so that there is a miscarriage, and yet no harm follows, the one who hurt her shall be fined, according as the woman's husband shall lay upon him; and he shall pay as the judges determine. If any harm follows, then you shall give life for life, eye for eye, tooth for tooth, hand for hand, foot for foot, burn for burn, wound for wound, stripe for stripe.

These penalties sound horrifying to modern ears, but they were in fact intended to set a limit to personal vengeance. It was an eye for an eye, and *no more*. There is also a clear distinction between punishment for offences against people (which are severe) and offences against property (which are much lighter), stressing the value of even the humblest individual.

Jesus condemned the desire for personal revenge (as did the Old Testament law); but he clearly did not believe that there was never any case for punishment as a deserved penalty. When he predicted the destruction of Jerusalem, he spoke of it as a judgement which would come on the nation simply *because* it had refused to recognize and acknowledge God's Messiah. And he spoke these words not in a fit or temper, but with tears:

And when he drew near and saw the city he wept over it, saying, 'Would that even today you knew the things that make for peace! But now they are hid from your eyes. For the days shall come upon you, when your enemies will cast up a bank about you and surround you, and hem you in on every side, and dash you to the ground, you and your children within you, and they will not leave one stone upon another in you; *because* you did not know the time of your visitation.

⚠ **Animal sacrifice is unintelligible and revolting to the modern mind. How can we accept any theory about the death of Jesus which is based on it?**

Although most people in the Western world have never seen an animal being killed in sacrifice, the very idea of offering such sacrifices to any god seems either quite meaningless, or to imply primitive and unworthy ideas of God. It conveys the idea that God is angry with men and needs to be placated with offerings.

▷ In the long run it is no help to say that it does not matter whether or not we understand what animal sacrifices were all about, because these ideas play such a large part in the way in which Jesus and the early Christians interpreted the meaning of his death. If we exclude all ideas connected with animal sacrifice, we may be in danger of arriving at an interpretation which has little or no connection with the thinking of Jesus and the early Christians.

Leon Morris outlines the ideas associated with sacrifice in the Old Testament:

Throughout the world of antiquity sacrifice was the almost universal religious rite. Among the Jews the procedure was as follows. A man would take along an animal to the altar, lay his hands on its head and then solemnly kill it. The priest would collect the blood, sprinkle some of it in a prescribed manner and pour the rest of it at the base of the altar. Then he would take certain prescribed parts of the animal (the whole of it in the case of the burnt sacrifice) and offer it to

God in the flames of the altar. Finally the priest would dispose of the rest of the carcase according to the rules governing the particular sacrifice being offered. Sacrifice might express homage to God, or fellowship before God with other worshippers, or it might be concerned with the expiation of sin.

▷ When we do understand the idea of animal sacrifice in the Old Testament, we may discover that the real reason why we find it repulsive is that it is associated with certain assumptions which we do not *like*. We may not like the idea that our proud independence of God, or our rebellion against him and his standards, call forth a certain reaction from him. We may not like the idea that, since we have grown up saying 'No!' to him in this life and refusing to accept him, we deserve to forfeit fellowship with him. We would like to believe that our refusal to love him and obey him is not as serious as the Bible would make us believe, and that we do not deserve such treatment from him. We may not *like* these assumptions very much; but we can hardly say that we do not *understand* them when they are clearly explained. Death *is* repulsive. The sacrifices serve as a visual aid in helping us to understand the death of Jesus.

⚠ Isn't the idea of someone dying in our place unjust?

Lord Byron:

The basis of your religion is injustice; the Son of God, the pure, the immaculate, the innocent is sacrificed for the guilty. This proves *His* heroism; but no more does away with *man's* guilt than a schoolboy's volunteering to be flogged for another would exculpate the dunce from negligence or preserve him from the rod.

▷ This objection rests partly on a misunderstanding. The New Testament never suggests that God the Father 'used' Jesus as an unwilling victim in order to vent his fury and rage on him instead of on the whole human race. There is no suggestion that God is like a teacher who is confronted with a disobedient class, and because he cannot punish the whole class, picks out one innocent person and punishes him. The New Testament writers stress that the whole process of reconciliation from start to finish was motivated by the love of God (i.e. of God the Father, God the Son and God the Holy Spirit). And when God the Son willingly went to the cross, this was God's way of expressing his hatred of sin and his love for the sinner at the same time. When we say, therefore, that Jesus bore our sins, we are saying that *God himself* has borne the consequences of our sins. There is no unwilling third party who is used as a scapegoat.

Paul shows how closely he related the work of Jesus to the work of God the Father when he speaks of

the church of God which he (i.e. God) purchased with his own blood.

▷ The objection may in some cases spring from human pride. Even admitting our need to be saved from the judgement of God, we would naturally prefer to find our own way of making our peace with him, a way by which we could take most of the credit for ourselves, or a way which would not cost us a great deal. It is therefore humiliating for us to be told that we cannot save ourselves, and that only God can save us.

▷ If we look at the alternatives, they are even less acceptable:

either we must hope that God will not after all give us what we deserve, or that he will disregard his laws;

or we must be prepared to remain guilty and bear the full consequences ourselves.

⚠ How can the death of one man in the first century deal with the sins of the whole human race?

That is to say:

How can the death of *one* man have this effect for *all* men?

How can *suffering and death* deal with *sin*?

How can his death *then* deal with my sins *now*?

▷ The answer to the first part of the question lies in the *identity* of the person who died. The death of an ordinary man could not have this effect for all men. But when the person who dies is the eternal Son of God, his death is unique and has unique effects. For if Jesus was the eternal Son of God, then what *Jesus* did, *God* did. We must not think of Jesus merely as a neutral third party coming between God and man. This is why Paul links God the Father so closely with Christ when he says:

God was in Christ reconciling the world to himself, not counting their trespasses against them . . .

The biblical understanding of the solidarity of the human race helps further to explain how the action of Jesus can affect all men. Adam is seen as the first man and the 'head' of the human race. All his descendants are thought of as being 'in Adam', and inherit his fallen human nature. Jesus, on the other hand, is seen as the 'second Adam' who reverses the effects of Adam's disobedience. All who believe in Christ are now no longer 'in Adam' and doomed to condemnation, but are 'in Christ' and enjoy a new relationship with God. And just as the disobedience of the *one* man Adam affected *all* men, so the obedience of the *one* man Jesus affects *all* who trust in him. This is how Paul draws out the parallel between Adam and Christ:

. . . sin came into the world through one man and death through sin, and so death spread to all men because all men sinned . . . But the free gift is not like the trespass. For if many died through one man's trespass, much more have the grace of God and the free gift in the grace of that one man Jesus Christ abounded for many. And the free gift is not like the effect of that one man's sin. For the judgement following one trespass brought condemnation, but the free gift following many trespasses brings justification. If, because of one man's trespass, death reigned through that one man, much more will those who receive the abundance of grace and the free gift of righteousness reign in life through the one man Jesus Christ.

▷ The answer to the second question similarly hinges on the *identity* of the man who suffered and died. It was not the *intensity* of the suffering which had the effect of dealing with sin, but its quality and value. It was not *how much* he suffered which makes the difference; it is rather *who* suffered, and the fact that death is so closely associated with sin in the Bible. (See p. 50.)

Moreover, the suffering and death of Jesus must not be isolated from his whole life. Sin came into the world through the *disobedience* of Adam, and the consequences of this disobedience could therefore only be undone through *obedience*—obedience exemplified not only in an isolated act, but throughout a life. In this way the willingness of Jesus to go to the cross is seen as the climax of a life which was utterly obedient to God. Paul writes:

Then as one man's trespass led to condemnation for all men, so one man's act of righteousness leads to acquittal and life for all men. For as by one man's disobedience many were made sinners, so by one man's obedience many will be made righteous.

▷ We must not think of the death of Jesus simply as a transaction carried out in the past. The New Testament writers speak of something that was accomplished when Jesus died on the cross. But the benefits of what he achieved do not pass to us automatically; we have to receive them by a conscious and deliberate act of faith. The fact that Jesus died so many years ago is hardly relevant; all that is relevant is that he died at a particular time in history, and that his death achieved salvation once and for all. His death does not need to be repeated in each generation, even if it could be.

He has appeared once for all at the end of the age to put away sin by the sacrifice of himself.

When Christ had offered for all time a single sacrifice for sins, he sat down at the right hand of God . . . For by a single offering he has perfected for all time those who are sanctified.

What Jesus achieved in the past has to be appropriated by each person in the present; and it is simply faith and trust in Jesus which makes the connection between the death and resurrection of Jesus in the past and our experience in the present. Paul writes:

Since we are justified by faith, we have peace with God through our Lord Jesus Christ. Through him we have obtained access to this grace in which we stand, and we rejoice in our hope of sharing the glory of God.

⚠ Isn't it inconceivable that a prophet sent from God should suffer and die in this way?

If a man is sent from God as a prophet, he has the authority of God behind him, and he represents God to the people. Is it conceivable that God should allow his messenger to undergo such humiliation and rejection? Surely God would intervene to save his representative from such a degrading fate.

This was probably *Peter's* feeling when he protested at the suggestion of Jesus having to suffer and die:

And Peter took him and began to rebuke him, saying, 'God forbid, Lord! This shall never happen to you.'

▷ **Judaism** has generally reacted in precisely the same way as Peter did, finding it inconceivable that God should have a 'Son', or that he should allow him to be killed without intervening.

The Jewish Encyclopedia:

'My God, my God . . .' which showed that even his resolute spirit had been daunted by the ordeal. This last utterance was in all its implications itself a disproof of the exaggerated claims made for him after his death by his disciples. The very form of his punishment would disprove those claims in Jewish eyes. No Messiah that Jews could recognize could suffer such a death; for 'He that is hanged is accursed of God' (Deut. 21: 23), 'an insult to God' (Targum, Rashi).

Hans Joachim Schoeps:

It is an impossible article of belief, which detracts from God's sovereignty and absolute otherness— an article which, in fact, destroys the world . . . It is the same passionate belief which can be heard in an admittedly late homiletical midrash: 'It is not permitted a human mouth to say, "The Holy One—blessed be he—has a son." If God could not look on in anguish while Abraham sacrificed his son, would he then have suffered his own son to be killed, without destroying the entire world?'

▷ It is clear from the Gospels that *Jesus* himself felt the full force of this kind of thinking. He must have felt its attraction very keenly, but rejected it because he knew that it was a purely human way of thinking which was not in accordance with the mind of God. He answered Peter very sternly:

Then Jesus turned and said to Peter, 'Away with you, Satan; you are a stumbling-block to me. You think as men think, not as God thinks.'

When Jesus realized what kind of death lay ahead of him, he knew that it was possible for him to appeal to God for deliverance; but he firmly rejected the idea:

Now is my soul troubled. And what shall I say, 'Father, save me from this hour'? No, for this purpose I have come to this hour . . .

When Peter began using a sword to protect Jesus, Jesus rebuked him and explained why he rejected the use of force to defend himself and why he refused to ask for a miraculous deliverance:

Then Jesus said to him, 'Put your sword back into its place; for all who take the sword will perish by the sword. Do you think that I cannot appeal to my Father, and he will at once send me more than twelve legions of angels? But how then should the scriptures be fulfilled, that it must be so?'

After his resurrection Jesus explained to the disciples that it was *necessary* for him to suffer in this way:

'O foolish men, and slow of heart to believe all that the prophets have spoken! Was it not necessary that the Christ should suffer these things and enter into his glory?' And beginning with Moses and all the prophets, he interpreted to them in all the scriptures the things concerning himself.

Then he opened their minds to understand the scriptures, and said to them, 'Thus it is written, that the Christ should suffer and on the third day rise from the dead, and that repentance and forgiveness of sins should be preached in his name to all nations . . .'

The many Old Testament passages from which Jesus explained the need for his suffering and death must have been the main source of understanding for the New Testament writers.

▷ **Islam.** It is probably this same assumption that God could not allow his prophet to suffer and die in this way that lies behind the

Qur'an's statements about the death of Jesus:

They denied the truth and uttered a monstrous falsehood against Mary. They declared: 'We have put to death the Messiah Jesus the son of Mary, the apostle of Allah.' They did not kill him, nor did they crucify him, but they thought they did.
   Those that disagreed about him were in doubt concerning his death, for what they knew about it was sheer conjecture; they were not sure that they had slain him. Allah lifted him up to his presence; He is mighty and wise.

   We need to be clear as to what precisely the Qur'an denies and what it does not deny:

   It does *not deny* that men wanted to kill Jesus.

   It does *not deny* that Jesus was willing to suffer and die.

   It *does deny* that Jesus was finally killed on the cross.

Dr Kenneth Cragg explains the background to this belief, and the traditional interpretations in Islam:

The context of controversy and dispute here referred to may reflect certain docetic tendencies in early heretical Christianity which, for various mainly metaphysical reasons, questioned the possibility of the Messiah being literally and actually a sufferer. The attitudes of Islam reproduce many of these misgivings and may derive from them historically . . .
   The prevailing view is that at some point, undetermined, in the course of the final events of Christ's arrest, trial and sentence, a substitute person replaced Him while Jesus Himself was, in the phrase, raised or raptured into Heaven, from whence, unscathed and uncrucified, He returned to His disciples in personal appearances in which He commissioned them to take His teachings out into the world. The Gospel they were thus to preach was a moral law only and not the good tidings of a victorious, redemptive encounter with sin and death. Meanwhile, the substitute sufferer bore the whole brunt of the historical crucifixion, having been sentenced and condemned *as if he were the Christ.*

▷The Moslem argues that the death of Jesus is unthinkable because it is *unnecessary* from God's point of view. The Christian answer must therefore be to seek to explain as far as possible *why* it was necessary for Christ to die (see pp.49ff). Some further points are worth making here:

—Forgiveness by its very nature involves suffering. The essence of forgiveness is that you accept an injury or an offence without wanting to punish or to fight back. You simply bear the injury and accept all the consequences. If this is true on the human level, the Christian would say that it is also true when we think about God forgiving men. When he forgives men the wrongs and injuries they have done to him, he himself is bearing the personal affront. In a sense he is taking the consequences upon himself. The Moslem, on the other hand, feels that God's forgiveness has little in common with forgiveness between men, and is more like the pardon extended by an all-powerful ruler to his subjects.

—If we can say that 'Christ . . . died for sins once for all . . . that he might bring us to God . . .' (1 Peter 3: 18), then it is possible to be *sure* that if we repent, we have been forgiven. Assurance of forgiveness is therefore based on what Jesus has already accomplished through his death. According to the Moslem way of thinking forgiveness depends entirely on our repentance and on God's mercy, which in turn depends on what happens on the Day of Judgement, when our good deeds are weighed in the balance against our bad deeds. This means we cannot be sure, here and now, of God's forgiveness, or of our final acceptance by him.

—If Jesus did not die, then he ceased to be identified with men at the point which men fear and dread most of all. And if Jesus did not die, he could not in any sense defeat and overcome death. If there was no death, there can have been no resurrection. Yet the writer of the letter to the Hebrews speaks in the clearest terms of Jesus destroying the power of death through his own death:

Since . . . the children share in flesh and blood he himself likewise partook of the same nature, that through death he might destroy him who has the power of death, that is, the devil, and deliver all those who through fear of death were subject to lifelong bondage.

"Did Jesus rise from the dead?"

The question we are asking here is a question about historical fact. Did Jesus rise from the dead or did he not? Did the resurrection really happen?

The evidence in the Gospels rests on the accounts of the empty tomb and of the appearances of the risen Jesus, and on the existence of the Christian church.

THE ACCOUNTS OF THE EMPTY TOMB

Christ's death

Jesus was nailed to the cross at about 9 a.m. on the Friday. Many were present when he died at about 3 p.m. (Mark 15: 21–37). John (19: 31–37) records that a Roman soldier 'stabbed his side with a lance, and at once there was a flow of blood and water.'

His burial

Soon after he died, Joseph of Arimathea, a member of the Jewish Council, received permission from Pilate, the Roman Governor, to take the body off the cross. He and Nicodemus (also a member of the Council) wrapped it with spices in strips of linen cloth and laid it in Joseph's unused tomb, which had been cut out of the rock in a garden very close to the site of the crucifixion. The women who had followed Jesus watched all this being done (Mark 15: 40–47; John 19: 38–42).

The guard

On the Saturday morning, the chief priests and Pharisees went to Pilate to ask him to have the tomb guarded, in case the disciples stole the body. Pilate agreed to this, and the tomb was then sealed and guarded by Roman soldiers (Matthew 27: 62–66).

The women at the tomb

Very early on the Sunday morning some of the women came to the tomb bringing more spices to anoint the body of Jesus, and they found that the stone had been rolled away from the entrance to the tomb. When they went inside they saw two angels who explained that Jesus had risen from the dead, and told them he would meet them again in Galilee (Mark 16: 1–8; Luke 24: 1–11).

The disciples at the tomb

The women hurried back to tell the disciples, and Peter and John ran to the tomb to see for themselves. John records that they saw 'the linen cloths lying, and the napkin, which had been on his head, not lying with the linen cloths but rolled up in a place by itself' (John 20: 1–10).

A good example of a rock tomb from the first century. The circular stone was rolled down a slight incline into place across the entrance.

THE ACCOUNTS OF THE APPEARANCES OF THE RISEN JESUS

▷ Mary returned to the tomb with Peter and John, and remained there after they had gone back. She stooped to look into the tomb again, and after speaking to the two angels, she turned round and saw Jesus, though at first she did not recognize him. He told her not to cling to him and gave her a message for the disciples (John 20: 11–18).

▷ On the same day, when two of the disciples were on their way to a village called Emmaus, about seven miles from Jerusalem, 'Jesus himself drew near and went with them. But their eyes were kept from recognizing him.' They talked with him about all that had happened and invited him to spend the night with them. As he broke the bread at table, 'they recognized him; and he vanished out of their sight'. They immediately returned to Jerusalem to tell the other disciples (Luke 24: 13–33).

▷ When they got back to the disciples, they were told that Jesus had appeared to Peter, and they gave their account of how Jesus had appeared to them on the road (Luke 24: 34–35).

▷ While they were talking about all this, 'Jesus himself stood among them. But they were startled and frightened and supposed that they saw a spirit. And he said to them, "Why are you troubled, and why do questionings rise in your hearts? See my hands and my feet, that it is I myself; handle me, and see; for a spirit has not flesh and bones as you see that I have." ' They were still unconvinced, and to give them further evidence he took a piece of fish and ate it in front of them (Luke 24: 36–49).

▷ On the following Sunday he appeared to

The Garden Tomb in Jerusalem, a typical rock tomb from the time of Jesus. The body was tightly bound in yards of linen dressed with spices, and laid on the slab (broken here). The head was also bound.

them again in the upper room. Thomas had not been present the previous week and was still sceptical about what the others told him; but now he was with them. 'The doors were shut, but Jesus came and stood among them.' He invited Thomas to touch his hands and his side (John 20: 24–29).

▷ Some time later he appeared to the disciples beside the Lake of Galilee, where he had spent much of the three years of his ministry. He had prepared a charcoal fire at the lakeside and had breakfast with them (John 21: 1–9).

▷ He appeared to them on another occasion on a mountain in Galilee, and gave them the commission, 'Go therefore and make disciples of all nations' (Matthew 28: 16–20).

▷ During this period also 'he appeared to more than 500 brethren at one time . . . then he appeared to James, then to all the apostles' (1 Corinthians 15: 3–8; Paul writing in about AD 57).

▷ The last occasion on which the disciples saw him was on the Mount of Olives in Jerusalem, about forty days after the resurrection (Acts 1: 6–11).

This is Luke's summary (in Acts 1: 3) of the period after the resurrection:

He showed himself to these men after his death, and gave ample proof that he was alive: over a period of forty days he appeared to them and taught them about the kingdom of God.

THE EXISTENCE OF THE CHRISTIAN CHURCH

The writer of the Acts of the Apostles describes the origin and spread of the Christian church. According to his account, the very fact that Christianity became a separate religion is part of the evidence for the resurrection.

The transformation of the disciples

When Jesus was arrested at night in the Garden of Gethsemane, the disciples all forsook him and fled. Peter followed at a distance while Jesus was led away for trial, and disowned him three times; he was apparently too ashamed or too afraid to be

Beside the Lake of Galilee, where Jesus spent much of his three-year ministry, and where he met his disciples after the resurrection.

The Mount of Olives, scene of the ascension of Jesus.

identified with Jesus now that he was being tried as a criminal. After the public execution of Jesus, the disciples all hid for a time in a locked room in Jerusalem, because they were still afraid of the Jewish authorities.

Seven weeks after the death of Jesus, however, a dramatic change came over the disciples. They were now no longer ashamed to be identified with Jesus, but were speaking about him boldly in public. When this brought them into open conflict with the Jewish authorities, they were prepared to be imprisoned and flogged rather than be forced to disown Jesus or to keep quiet about him (Acts 2 – 4).

The separation of Christianity from Judaism

When *the disciples* first began to speak boldly about Jesus on the Day of Pentecost, they laid special emphasis on the resurrection and the implications of the resurrection. They never ceased to think of themselves as Jews, but it was their persistent teaching of this message about Jesus and the resurrection which led to persecution from the Jewish authorities (Acts 4: 1–22).

This same pattern was repeated in the life of *Paul*, who had been brought up as a devout Jew and thoroughly trained in the school of the Pharisees. He took an active part in the persecution of Christians, but in about AD 34 or 35 he himself became a Christian and his preaching about Jesus and the resurrection soon brought him into conflict with the Jewish authorities.

Luke, the author of Acts, was writing for a Roman called Theophilus, who probably wanted to know how Christianity had come into being, how it differed from Judaism, and in particular why Paul was on trial in Rome. He therefore describes in considerable detail how he came to be a prisoner in Rome, and in doing so illustrates the final breach between Christianity and Judaism.

He tells us that in many places Jews opposed Paul and his message and often actively persecuted him. Eventually some of them plotted to murder him, and were about to kill him during a disturbance in the Temple area in Jerusalem, when he was rescued by Roman soldiers. The Roman authorities arranged for him to be tried before the Jewish Council, the same Council which had condemned Jesus and handed him over for execution about thirty years before. In the course of the trial he argued (Acts 23: 6):

The true issue in this trial is our hope of the resurrection of the dead.

What he was saying to them in effect was this: 'Those of you who are Pharisees believe in the future resurrection; and you who are Sadducees say that the resurrection is impossible. We Christians believe in a future resurrection, and we also believe that Jesus has already been raised from the dead. The basic issue in this trial therefore is simply this: did it happen or did it not? Was Jesus raised from the dead or was he not?'

Luke clearly wanted his readers to understand that it was belief in the resurrection of Jesus which was the basic issue dividing Christianity from Judaism, and for which Paul was on trial (Acts 21: 27 – 28: 31).

Luke also tells us (Acts 17: 16–32) that it was Paul's insistence on the resurrection which roused the curiosity and the scorn of the philosophers in Athens:

Some said, 'What would this babbler say?' Others said, 'He seems to be a preacher of foreign divinities'—because he preached Jesus and the resurrection . . . Now when they heard of the resurrection of the dead, some mocked; but others said, 'We will hear you again about this.'

Since we are asking a historical question (did Jesus rise from the dead or did he not?), we need to approach the above evidence in the same way as we would for other historical questions.

But since we are dealing with something unique, it is essential to be aware of our own assumptions. It is not quite as simple as a Sherlock Holmes detective case. Our assumptions will play an important part in our estimate of what is possible or impossible in history. If we approach the evidence with our minds *already made up* that miracles *cannot* happen, no amount of evidence will convince us that the resurrection *did* happen. If on the other hand we are prepared to believe that there is a God who can work miracles in the universe he has made, then we may be willing to be convinced—provided, of course, the evidence is good enough.

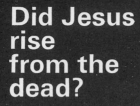

Did Jesus rise from the dead?

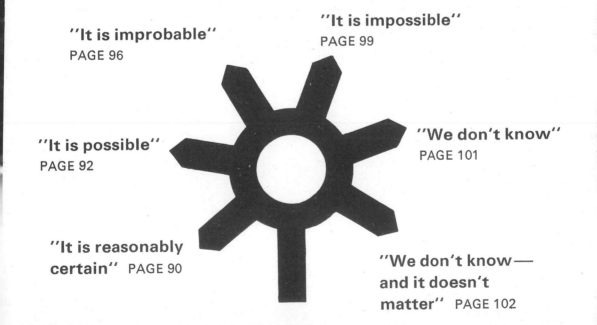

"It is improbable"
PAGE 96

"It is impossible"
PAGE 99

"It is possible"
PAGE 92

"We don't know"
PAGE 101

"It is reasonably certain" PAGE 90

"We don't know— and it doesn't matter" PAGE 102

ANSWER 1: BIBLICAL CHRISTIANITY

"It is reasonably certain that Jesus rose from the dead"

This is to say, although we cannot objectively prove the resurrection with 100 per cent certainty, we have sufficient evidence to be reasonably certain that it did happen. There are good grounds for believing that Jesus rose from the dead.

If you give this answer, the next obvious step is to consider what the resurrection means. If the event has no significance there is no point in pursuing the enquiry any further. We might just as well conclude that it did not happen.

These are some of the conclusions which the early Christians drew from the resurrection:

It provides conclusive evidence about the identity of Jesus. All that Jesus had claimed about himself is vindicated by the resurrection.

Peter speaking to the crowds in Jerusalem on the Day of Pentecost:

This Jesus God raised up, and of that we all are witnesses . . . Let all the house of Israel therefore know assuredly that God has made him both Lord and Christ, this Jesus whom you crucified.

It vindicates the work of Jesus and demonstrates that his death achieved something. If he had not been raised from death, his death would have been evidence of the failure of his mission. This is how the risen Jesus himself interpreted the meaning of his death:

These are my words which I spoke to you, while I was still with you, that everything written about me in the law of Moses and the prophets

and the psalms must be fulfilled . . . Thus it is written, that the Christ should suffer and on the third day rise from the dead, and that repentance and forgiveness of sins should be preached in his name to all nations.

It makes Jesus the perfect mediator who brings us into fellowship with the Father. The risen Christ gives us the right to come to the Father with boldness and confidence.

Through him (Jesus) we . . . have access in one Spirit to the Father.

He is able for all time to save those who draw near to God through him, since he always lives to make intercession for them.

It can mean something in everyday experience. For the Christian the resurrection is not simply an event in the past to which he looks back. It also has implications for the present.

The person who puts his trust in Jesus is united with him; and this union and identification with him offers a real deliverance from the power of sin, and an opportunity of enjoying here and now a 'newness of life' which flows from Christ's own risen life. If we are now 'in Christ' and are willing to die to self as he did, all the benefits of his death and resurrection are available to us.

We were buried therefore with him by baptism into death, so that as Christ was raised from the dead by the glory of the Father, we too might walk in newness of life. For if we have been united with him in a death like his, we shall certainly be united with him in a resurrection like his. We know that our old self was crucified with him so that the sinful body might be destroyed, and we might no longer be enslaved to sin. For he who has died is freed from sin. But if we have died with Christ, we believe that we shall also live with him. For we know that Christ being raised from the dead will never die again; death no longer has dominion over him. The death he died he died to sin, once for all, but the life he lives he lives to God. So you also must consider yourselves dead to sin and alive to God in Christ Jesus.

I count everything as loss because of the surpassing worth of knowing Christ Jesus my Lord. For his sake I have suffered the loss of all things, and count them as refuse, in order that I may gain Christ . . . that I may know him and the power of his resurrection, and may share in his sufferings, becoming like him in his death, that if possible I may attain the resurrection from the dead.

None of us lives to himself, and none of us dies to himself. If we live, we live to the Lord, and if we die, we die to the Lord; so then, whether we live or whether we die, we are the Lord's. For to this end Christ died and lived again, that he might be Lord both of the dead and of the living.

The power by which God raised Jesus from death is available still. In desperate situations the Christian can have confidence that God is still able to work in the same dynamic way. Paul makes it plain that this confidence is no mere wishful thinking:

. . . we do not want you to be ignorant, brethren, of the affliction we experienced in Asia; for we were so utterly, unbearably crushed that we despaired of life itself. Why, we felt that we had received the sentence of death; but that was to make us rely not on ourselves but on God who raises the dead; he delivered us from so deadly a peril, and he will deliver us; on him we have set our hope that he will deliver us again.

It means that Jesus has triumphed over death. The believer will share this victory, and even now can enjoy the confidence and peace which this gives:

Our Saviour Christ Jesus . . . abolished death and brought life and immortality to light through the gospel.

Blessed be the God and Father of our Lord Jesus Christ! By his great mercy we have been born anew to a living hope through the resurrection of Jesus Christ from the dead.

Since . . . the children share in flesh and blood, he himself likewise partook of the same nature, that through death he might destroy him who has the power of death, that is, the devil, and deliver all those who through fear of death were subject to lifelong bondage.

Lo! I tell you a mystery. We shall not all sleep, but we shall all be changed, in a moment, in the twinkling of an eye, at the last trumpet. For the trumpet will sound, and the dead will be raised imperishable, and we shall be changed. For this perishable nature must put on the imperishable, and this mortal nature must put on immortality. When the perishable puts on the imperishable, and the mortal puts on immortality, then shall be brought to pass the saying that is written: 'Death is swallowed up in victory.' 'O death, where is thy victory? O death, where is thy sting?'

If you believe that it is probable or reasonably certain that Jesus was raised from the dead, and that these are some of the implications of the resurrection, then you should go on to consider what it means to be a Christian and to enter into a personal relationship with the living Christ. (See further 'Where do we go from here?' pp. 111ff.)

ANSWER 2

"It is possible that Jesus rose from the dead"

This is to say, we cannot rule out the possibility that the resurrection happened; we just cannot be certain.

If you think that the resurrection *could* possibly have happened, but are still unable to decide definitely for yourself one way or the other, then your final answer will probably depend on further examination of the evidence. You can sift the evidence by asking such questions as these and considering all the possible answers.

How are we to account for the story of the empty tomb?

These are all the theories which have been suggested:

Jesus was not really dead. The theory goes that Jesus was not really dead when he was taken down from the cross. Some time after being placed in the cool tomb he revived and got out of the tomb.

BUT: after being scourged and hanging on the cross for six hours, Jesus would have needed considerable medical treatment. Is it likely that a person in such a condition (with his back lacerated by a scourging that often proved fatal, with wounds in his hands and feet and a sword-thrust in his side) could appear to people who had known him well, *and* give the impression that he had been raised from death?

We are told that the body of Jesus was wrapped in long pieces of cloth and covered with a large amount of spices. He would have had to extricate himself from these graveclothes, roll aside the heavy stone which

several women feared they would be unable to move and escape the notice of the guard.

If he didn't really die at this time, what happened to him afterwards? How did he finally die?

The women came to the wrong tomb. It is argued that in the dim light of the early morning the women went to a different tomb, which was empty.

BUT: we are told that the women watched Joseph and Nicodemus taking the body and putting it in the tomb on the Friday evening.

The disciples went to the tomb after hearing the report of the women; are we to assume that they were all misled, and that they did nothing to check up on the facts?

When Joseph of Arimathea heard the rumours about the resurrection, wouldn't he have taken the trouble to check the facts for himself, since he had put the corpse in his own tomb in his private garden?

What about the detailed description of the way in which the graveclothes were lying? Must we assume this was invented?

The body could have been stolen.

BUT: who would have stolen it? And what motive could there be?

▷ It could have been the Roman authorities or the guards: but what possible motive could they have? It was in their own interests to see that the Jesus affair was closed.

▷ It could have been the Jewish authorities:

but again, what was the motive? If they knew (as Matthew tells us) that Jesus had prophesied that he would rise from the dead, they would want to ensure that the body did *not* disappear from the tomb, in case the disciples might claim that he had risen. Indeed, Matthew tells us that it was the Jewish authorities who asked for the guard to be placed at the tomb.

▷ It could have been an unknown person or group of people: but what was the motive? If the body was stolen by anyone who was not a disciple, could he not have produced the remains of the body as soon as the Christians began preaching about the resurrection? If he couldn't produce the remains, could he not at least come forward and provide enough evidence to convince many people that there was a perfectly natural explanation for what the disciples were talking about? Or must we fall back on the suggestion that it was done by an unknown person without any particular motive; that he let no one know what he had done, and left Jerusalem soon after stealing the body? No one can deny that this is a possible explanation; but is it likely?

▷ It could have been the disciples or some friends of Jesus (e.g. Joseph of Arimathea); but what possible motive was there? And does this tally with the rest of the account which tells us that the disciples were not expecting anything to happen? Would they not be putting themselves in a dangerous position with the authorities, who might give them the same treatment they had given Jesus? And if one or more of the friends of Jesus stole the body, how could they have concealed it from the others? If those who stole it remained Christians for the rest of their lives, their whole faith would have been based on a lie. We would also have to say that the other disciples were extraordinarily gullible in believing the story of the resurrection without checking up on the facts for themselves, and in being prepared to die for this incredible story.

The story has been exaggerated. On this theory, something miraculous may have happened, and the story may have some basis in fact. But we cannot accept all the details of the story, since there must have been some elaboration somewhere along the line.

BUT: how are we to decide what is fact and what is fiction in the accounts? By what principles are we to decide what really happened and what was added later on? Most of the suggested rules are very subjective and the dividing line is bound to be very delicate. The sceptic will naturally want to say, 'Why do you draw the line here? If you reject so much, why do you stop here and not reject some more?'

No vast period of time elapsed between the death of Jesus and the first written record which speaks about the resurrection—i.e. Paul's letter to the Corinthians, which was written about 26 years after the events.

It is natural to assume that the disciples and followers of Jesus would have gone to the tomb to check up on the rumours for themselves. And the more eyewitnesses there are to any event, the greater the safeguard against individuals elaborating the story.

The story was not passed on through a large number of people between the original eyewitnesses and the writers. It is not a fair comparison to say 'Look how much a story can get twisted and distorted when it passes from mouth to mouth. It comes out very different by the time it reaches the 50th person.'

When the first accounts were written, many of the original eyewitnesses would still have been alive, and could easily have confirmed the details of the story or cast doubt on them and discredited them. Luke, for one, specifically claims to have obtained information directly from eye-witnesses (Luke 1: 2).

The whole story has been invented. Nothing like this ever happened, so the argument goes. The body remained in the tomb, and the first disciples knew it. However, in the course of time they, and/or other Christians, came to express their faith in Jesus in terms of a story describing events. The story was not intended to be an historical account of what happened, but was merely intended as a way of expressing their beliefs about Jesus. Some would say that the stories were invented deliberately and consciously to convince others about the identity of Jesus. Others say that there was nothing dishonest about what they did, and that it would have been very natural for them to express their personal beliefs and experiences in this way.

BUT: if there was no event which led the disciples to their faith in the victory of Jesus over death, how did they come to believe this in the first place? If it was the faith of the early Christians which produced the story of the empty tomb, what gave them that faith?

One can imagine a person composing a myth to teach something or to stir the imagination; but why compose such a story (even with the best of motives) and present it as sober fact rather than as pure fantasy?

Even if the disciples had the very best motives in inventing the story, would they really be prepared to go on teaching it to others as simple fact when they found that it was just this which led to ridicule, persecution and suffering?

If the early Christians who used the story of the empty tomb understood it simply as myth and nothing more, why should anyone want to oppose their message?

What about the question of honesty? When is a lie not a lie? At some stage in the process there would inevitably have been many Christians (followers of one who claimed to be 'the truth') who knew perfectly well that the story of the empty tomb was not true, but went on telling the story which led others to believe that something objective really did happen.

The documents are reliable. If the theories outlined above seem unconvincing, there remains only one alternative—that the New Testament documents are reliable. They give us an account (though not an exhaustive one) of what the disciples actually witnessed.

How are we to account for the stories of the appearances of the risen Jesus?

Hallucination. There was never anyone there; the disciples were simply experiencing some kind of hallucination.

BUT: although individuals can experience hallucination, a group of people who have very different personalities normally do not. It is virtually unheard of for 500 people to experience the same kind of hallucination

at the same time.

These experiences were reported over a period of seven weeks and were not confined to one day; and they occurred at different places and at different times of the day.

Hallucination often takes the form of seeing things one would like to see; but there is no evidence that the disciples were expecting or looking for these appearances.

Exaggeration. There was something there, but the details have been exaggerated.

BUT: as before (see p. 93), how are we to decide what happened? How are we to pare away the additions from the accounts as they stand?

Nothing really happened. Nothing actually happened in the objective world; the disciples either *saw visions* communicated to them by God or had *experiences which were purely subjective*. Eventually they came to express these experiences and their new beliefs about Jesus in terms of stories about seeing, hearing and touching the risen Jesus. They were so conscious of the continuing influence of his personality and teaching, that they came to express this in terms of 'myth'—i.e. the stories looked as if they were about real events in the external world, but in fact they were merely a convincing way of expressing personal beliefs about Jesus.

BUT: exactly the same problems arise as before (see p. 93 above).

The accounts are factual and reliable. The documents together give us an account of *what the disciples* actually witnessed—what they saw with their eyes, heard with their ears and touched with their hands. The accounts are not exhaustive; they do not tell us, for instance, what the risen Christ was wearing. But they are detailed enough to rule out the idea that the appearances were purely inward, subjective experiences, or that the disciples were merely seeing some kind of ghost.

How are we to account for the existence of the Christian church?

If we discount the evidence of the New Testament about the origin of the Christian

After Jesus' death and resurrection the disciples met and taught in 'Solomon's Portico'. These arches are in the position of the porticos which surrounded the Temple courtyard in New Testament times.

church, how did it come into existence?

> How are we to explain the transformation of the small group of frightened disciples?

> How are we to account for the separation of Christianity from Judaism?

According to the Gospels and Acts, it was the resurrection which transformed the disciples. Because of their conviction about the risen Christ, they had the courage to abandon their defensive position and to tell the world the good news of his death and resurrection. The records imply that if they had been content to speak about Jesus simply as a good man or a prophet or teacher, they would never have brought on themselves such fierce opposition and suffering. The Jews would never have had any reason to persecute the Christians, and they would probably have remained as a small sect within Judaism. In this case, Christianity would never have become a separate religion.

For each of these questions you must simply decide for yourself which answer best fits the facts. This kind of examination of the evidence should therefore lead you to one of the other possible answers:

> reasonably certain (p. 90)

> improbable (p. 96)

> don't know (p. 101)

ANSWER 3

"It is improbable that Jesus rose from the dead"

This is to say, it is not impossible that something extraordinary happened, but the evidence is far from convincing. There are other possible and far more plausible explanations of what is recorded in the Gospels.

The Jewish Encyclopedia suggests that the belief in the resurrection is

. . . due to two psychic forces that never before had come so strongly into play: (1) the great personality of Jesus, which had so impressed itself upon the simple people of Galilee as to become a living power to them even after his death; and (2) the transcendentalism, or other-worldliness, in which those penance-doing, saintly men and women of the common classes, in their longing for godliness, lived . . . In an atmosphere of such perfect naiveté the miracle of the Resurrection seemed as natural as had been the miracle of the healing of the sick.

Hugh Schonfield has put forward his theory of the 'Passover Plot'. He suggests that Jesus planned secretly with a few friends (but not with his disciples) that he should be taken down from the cross before he died, so that he could be revived later. They were to give the impression, however, that he was really dead. In the event, the plot failed; for although he was not completely dead when he was taken down from the cross, he died soon afterwards before he could be revived. In spite of the failure of the plot, Schonfield sees a profound meaning in these events:

He had schemed in faith for his physical recovery, and what he expected had been frustrated by circumstances quite beyond his control. Yet when he sank into sleep, his faith was unimpaired, and by an extraordinary series of contributory events, partly resulting from his own planning,

it proved to have been justified. In a manner he had not forseen resurrection had come to him . . .
. . . Whenever mankind strives to bring in the rule of justice, righteousness and peace, there the deathless presence of Jesus the Messiah is with them.

Everyone knows that the revolutionary leader Ché Guevara is dead. Yet his followers still use the slogan 'Ché Lives!'

Ronald Gregor Smith believes that the historical evidence for the resurrection is altogether unconvincing; but he goes on to say that this does not destroy Christian faith:

So far as historicity is concerned, . . . it is neces-sary to explain: we may freely say that the bones of Jesus lie somewhere in Palestine.

Christian faith is not destroyed by this admission. On the contrary, only now, when this has been said, are we in a position to ask about the meaning of the resurrection as an integral part of the message concerning Jesus.

POINTS TO CONSIDER ABOUT THIS ANSWER

▷ If you give this kind of answer, you still have to account for the very strong *belief* in the resurrection among the early Christians. If you believe that nothing like the resurrection took place, you still ought to work out some theory to explain how it was that the disciples were misled, *or* how they came to be misleading others, *or* how we today (and the majority of Christians in the past) are misled when we read these stories as if they are an account of events which actually happened.

Many of those who say that the story is highly improbable refuse to work out a *detailed* alternative. But some who do, recognize how tentative it must be.

Hugh Schonfield:

We are nowhere claiming for our reconstruction that it represents what actually happened, but that on the evidence we have it may be fairly close to the truth . . .

Naturally it cannot be said that this is a solution to the puzzle (about the alleged appearances of Jesus after his death). . . . There is room for other theories, such as that the man concerned (i.e. the man who collaborated with Jesus in the Passover Plot), if there was one, was a medium, and that Jesus, rising from the dead into the After Life in the spiritualist sense, spoke through him in his own voice which enabled his presence to be recognized . . . Too little is told, and that little quickly became too legendary, and too contradictory, for any assured conclusion. The view taken here does seem to fit the requirements and is in keeping with what has been disclosed of the Passover Plot. The planning of Jesus for his expected recovery created the mystery of the empty tomb.

▷ If you give this kind of answer you ought to be completely consistent and draw the appropriate conclusions about Jesus (as the first writer does): that he was an ordinary man whose career was ended by a cruel death, and that he is no more 'alive' today than Socrates or Confucius or any other historical character.

You may want to say that Jesus' outlook on life is an appropriate one for people today to have. But there is nothing unique about making this kind of claim for a historical character. A nationalist in South America could speak in exactly the same way about Che Guevara, and a Chinese Communist might think in these terms about Mao Tse Tung. If you use the word 'resurrection' to describe the influence of Jesus and his life and teaching on you, you are confusing the issue. For you are giving the word a completely different meaning from the usual Christian one.

If you use the word 'resurrection', most people will automatically think of someone being raised from death. But this is not what you mean by the word, and there is bound to be an element of deception or misunderstanding if you continue to use the word. You ought in all fairness to find a different one (compare the similar problems in the ambiguous use of 'God', BOOK TWO, pp. 33ff.)

▷ The *meaning* of the resurrection can hardly survive without the *event* of the resurrection. If the resurrection did not happen, you cannot ask what the resurrection means. And to say that the meaning can survive without the event is rather like the story in Alice in Wonderland where the grin of the Cheshire Cat survives even after the Cat himself has slowly disappeared:

'All right,' said the Cat; and this time it vanished quite slowly, beginning with the end of the tail, and ending with the grin, which remained sometime after the rest of it had gone.

'Well! I've often seen a cat without a grin,' thought Alice; 'but a grin without a cat! It's the most curious thing I ever saw in all my life!'

In the end there may be little point in arguing about the details of the historical events. For your estimate of what is probable or improbable in history will be determined by your understanding of God and the universe. (See further BOOK TWO, Questions Two and Four, 'Who or what is God?' and 'What kind of universe do we live in?')

ANSWER 4

"It is impossible for Jesus to have risen from the dead"

This is to say, it is inconceivable that any human being should be raised from death. In the light of all that science has discovered about the workings of the universe, it is simply not possible for a dead man to be raised to life.

David Hume, the eighteenth-century Scottish philosopher, gave this kind of answer, and many answers given today are simply a restatement of his argument in a different form.

A miracle is a violation of the laws of nature; and as a firm and unalterable experience has established these laws, the proof against a miracle from the very nature of the fact, is as entire as any argument from experience can possibly be imagined. . . . It is a miracle, that a dead man should come to life; because that has never been observed in any age or country. There must therefore be a uniform experience against every miraculous event, otherwise the event would not merit that appellation. And as a uniform experience amounts to proof, there is here a direct and full *proof*, from the nature of the fact, against the existence of any miracle; nor can such a proof be destroyed, or the miracle rendered credible, but by an opposite proof, which is superior.

The plain consequence is . . . that no testimony is sufficient to establish a miracle, unless the testimony be of such kind, that its falsehood would be more miraculous, than the fact, which it endeavours to establish . . . When anyone tells me, that he saw a dead man restored to life, I immediately consider with myself, whether it be more probable, that this person should either deceive or be deceived, or that the fact, which he relates, should really have happened. I weigh the one miracle against the other; and according to the superiority, which I discover, I pronounce my decision, and always reject the greater miracle.

After discussing the evidence for certain miracles outside the Bible, but without discussing in detail the evidence for the resurrection, he concludes:

Upon the whole, then, it appears, that no testimony for any kind of miracle has ever amounted to a probability, much less to a proof; and that even supposing it amounted to a proof, it would be opposed by another proof . . . We may establish it as a maxim, that no human testimony can have such force as to prove a miracle, and make it a just foundation for any such system of religion.

His argument can be summarized in these stages:

> The uniformity of natural causes within a closed system is an established fact.
>
> No testimony about any miracle has ever been sufficiently convincing.
>
> Therefore miracles *cannot* happen.
>
> Therefore miracles *do not* happen, and the resurrection did not happen.

Hume draws the obvious conclusion that Christianity cannot be true.

C. S. Lewis summarizes Hume's argument in this way:

Ever since Hume's famous *Essay* it has been believed that historical statements about miracles are the most intrinsically improbable of all historical statements. According to Hume, probability rests on what may be called the majority vote of our past experiences. The more often a thing has been known to happen, the more probable it is that it should happen again; and the less often the less probable. Now the regularity of Nature's course, says Hume, is supported by something better than the majority vote of past experiences: it is supported by their unanimous vote, or, as Hume says, by 'firm and unalterabe experience'. Thereis, in fact, 'uniform experiencel' against Miracle; otherwise, says Hume, it would not be Miracle. A Miracle is therefore the most improbable of all events. It is always more probable that the witnesses were lying or mistaken than that a Miracle occurred.

POINTS TO CONSIDER ABOUT THIS ANSWER

▷ You still have to account for the strong *belief* in the resurrection among the early Christians. If you believe that the resurrection could not have happened, you still ought to find some way of explaining how it was that the disciples were misled, *or* how they came to be misleading others, *or* how we today (and the majority of Christians in the past) have been misled in assuming that these stories were intended to be taken at their face value as accounts of things that happened.

▷ In the end the real argument will not be about the details of the New Testament accounts, but about basic assumptions. If you approach the evidence with your mind already made up that no human being could ever be raised from death, then no amount of historical evidence will convince you.

C. E. M. Joad, writing at the time when he did not believe in the resurrection, explains how his presuppositions prevented him from taking the detailed evidence seriously:

The question at issue is . . . for me not so much a question of proving that the Christian record of fact is false or that the Christian revelation in the matter of the Resurrection cannot be substantiated; to a mind awake to the new knowledge of science these time-honoured claims you continue to make seem to be those of a man talking in his sleep.

To ascribe a central position to Jesus in the history of mankind may have accorded well enough with the narrow world picture of the Middle Ages, with its few thousand years of human history and its expectation of Christ's Return in the comparatively near future to put an end to the universe. But to me and to any modern this whole way of thinking is as unintelligible as it is impertinent. The framework of assumptions required for an understanding of the modern universe has been so widened that the old Christian hypothesis is lost sight of. And that, I suppose, is why, to return to your oft-reiterated complaint, we simply cannot be bothered to give the Christian hypothesis the attention which you seem to think it still deserves.

If therefore you would give an answer of this kind, you should consider some of the implications of this view of the universe. (See further BOOK TWO, Questions Two and Four, 'Who or what is God?' and 'What kind of universe do we live in?')

ANSWER 5

"We don't know whether or not Jesus rose from the dead"

This is to say, we cannot be sure one way or the other.
We simply do not know for certain.

POINTS TO CONSIDER ABOUT THIS ANSWER

▷ If it is a question of the *amount* of evidence available, how much *more* evidence would you demand before making up your mind? Are you demanding a degree of certainty which you would never dream of asking for other events which are supposed to have happened in the past? The resurrection of a dead man is obviously an extraordinary event; and you have every right to ask for convincing evidence before you commit yourself to believing that it happened. But are you asking for an impossible kind of historical proof?

▷ What *kind* of evidence do you think could be found which would enable you to give a more definite answer? Suppose, for example, a document were found which was written by a Roman or a Greek or a Jew, and which said that Jesus had been raised from death; what would it prove? It would prove that some people (perhaps including non-Christians) believed that Jesus did rise from death. But would it prove anything more than this? And in any case, would you not be able to find an easier way of explaining this evidence—by saying, for example, that

the document could have been a forgery, written by Christians to provide independent evidence?

The well-known passage from Josephus' *Antiquities* comes into this very category; since Josephus, the Jewish historian, was not a Christian. (See pp. 36 and 107.)

▷ Even supposing (for the sake of argument) that there were no evidence outside the New Testament for the resurrection, what would it prove? It could mean:

either   that the whole story was invented by Christians;

or   that of those who believed that it did happen, some became Christians and were content to believe the testimony of the eyewitnesses who were still alive, while others saw no significance in the event and saw no reason to write about it.

▷ If, after a detailed study of the evidence, you continue to give this answer, you should consider some of the consequences of consistent agnosticism (see BOOK ONE, pp.4 ff.)

ANSWER 6

"We don't know whether or not Jesus rose from the dead —and it doesn't matter"

This is to say, it is impossible to be certain whether the resurrection happened or not; but in any case, it doesn't really matter. Faith in Jesus Christ does not depend on the results of historical enquiry. For it is a personal faith, independent of questions about what actually happened.

To this way of thinking, therefore, in spite of the uncertainty,

either   we accept the resurrection by a leap of faith, knowing that it is contrary to reason;

or   we accept the resurrection as symbol or myth;

or   we remain content simply to experience what 'resurrection' means in our own lives.

Rudolph Bultmann:

The resurrection is not an event of past history. All that historical criticism can establish is the fact that the first disciples came to believe in the resurrection. The historian can perhaps to some extent account for that faith from the personal intimacy which the disciples had enjoyed with Jesus during his earthly life, and so reduce the resurrection appearances to a series of subjective visions. But the historical problem is scarcely relevant to Christian belief in the resurrection. For the historical event of the rise of the Easter faith means for us what it meant to the first disciples, namely, the self-manifestation of the risen Lord, the act of God in which the redemptive event of the cross is completed.

The resurrection of Jesus cannot be a miraculous proof by which the sceptic might be compelled to believe in Christ. The difficulty is not simply the incredibility of a mythical event like the resuscitation of a corpse—for that is what the resurrection means . . . Nor is it merely the

difficulty of establishing the objective historicity of the resurrection no matter how many witnesses are cited, as though once it was established it might be believed beyond question and might have its unimpeachable guarantee. No; the real difficulty is that the resurrection is itself an article of faith, and you cannot establish one article of faith because it is far more that the resuscitation of a corpse—it is an eschatological event. And so it cannot be a miraculous proof.

The resurrection is not a mythological event adduced in order to prove the saving efficacy of the cross, but an article of faith just as much as the meaning of the cross itself. Indeed, faith in the resurrection is really the same thing as faith in the saving efficacy of the cross, faith in the cross as the cross of Christ.

The real purpose of myth is not to present an objective picture of the world as it is, but to express man's understanding of himself in the world in which he lives. Myth should be interpreted not cosmologically, but anthropologically, or better still, existentially.

Harvey Cox is prepared to accept the assumptions of naturalistic science—i.e. the universe is a system in which there can be no divine intervention. He therefore admits that on these assumptions, the resurrection is not possible. He believes, however, that Christian faith can survive in spite of this contradiction:

We will have to live the rest of our lives both

with the affirmation that in some way the Christ lives among us and with the gnawing doubt that this really isn't possible. If we want to escape this kind of ambiguity, we are looking for a perfection which will not be available in this life.

I personally do not believe that we shall have any *personal* experience of the deep mystery . . . (of the resurrection) until we are ready to identify our lives with these people (the poor, the rejected, the despised, the sick and the hurt) in our time. Then and only then I think do we have the kind of experience on the basis of which we can talk about the reality of the resurrection.

Paul van Buren:

As historians, and indeed as proper users of the English language, we would prefer not to speak of the Easter event as a 'fact' at all, not in the ordinary sense of the word. We can say something about the situation before Easter, and we can say other things about the consequences of the Easter event, but the resurrection does not lend itself to being spoken of as a 'fact', for it cannot be described. We can say that

Jesus died and was buried, and that his disciples were then discouraged and disappointed men. That was the situation before Easter . . . On the other side of Easter, we can say that the disciples were changed men. They apparently found themselves caught up in something like the freedom of Jesus himself, having become men who were free to face even death without fear. Whatever it was that lay between, and which might account for this change, is not open to our historical investigation. The evidence is insufficient. All we can say is that something happened.

John Wren-Lewis:

The important thing about a myth or a fiction is the direction in which it points us, and for me the Christian myth of resurrection is important because it represents a vision of the possibility of building a world where love shall be all in all.

There is a real possibility . . . that the idea of resurrection might well be an expression of the ultimate achievements of technology.

POINTS TO CONSIDER ABOUT THIS ANSWER

▷ If you give this kind of answer, how do you justify your historical scepticism? Are you just as sceptical about other documents of the period—e.g. the writings of Roman historians and Josephus, the Jewish historian? Or is it merely the extraordinary content of the New Testament documents which makes you believe that they cannot be taken as straightforward records of what happened?

And why do you not carry your scepticism one stage further? What answer can you give to the person who refuses even to believe that the first disciples came to believe in the resurrection? How do you decide where to draw the line between what can be established by historical criticism and what must be left open?

▷ This kind of answer depends on certain assumptions, either about the nature of faith or about the universe:

Eduard Schweitzer declares the assumption

that only 'faith' can create faith:

Even if we had the best film of a Jerusalem newsreel of the year 30 AD (or whatever it was), it would not help us much since it could not show us what really happened on that day. Only Easter, the revelation of the Spirit, shows what really happened . . . Historical facts never create faith, only faith creates faith.

Proof cannot be given of Jesus' resurrection . . . God exposes himself to scepticism, doubt, and disbelief, renouncing anything that would compel men to believe.

The immediate effect of this conclusion is extremely liberating. The earliest Christians obviously cared astonishingly little about all the details of the Easter event—the where and how of it. But this means that the Easter faith does not depend on our success in believing in the possibility and historicity of all kinds of remarkable happenings, like the ability of the risen Lord to eat. It means, furthermore, that our assurance of Jesus' resurrection does not wax or wane depending on how precisely we read these accounts and on what new sources are discovered.

But if there are no guarantees for Easter faith, on what is our assurance based? . . .

When . . . assurance grows out of life with the word of the risen Lord and in obedience to him, the historical details of what happened at Easter become incidental. For faith no longer needs the guarantees of proof. To faith, the empty tomb will be a sign of what has taken place. It will not, however, fight for the empty tomb as for an article of faith, because the truth of Easter does not in fact depend on the empty tomb. What is important is whether the believer has such faith in the risen Lord that he will live under his dominion, will hold fast to the lordship of Jesus even when it leads him to his death. Only then will he find out whether he really relies on him 'who raises the dead' (2 Cor. 1. 8–9). And so the disciples, too, had to learn to understand what really took place at Easter through years of service under the living Christ, by living under his dominion and letting him show them what his resurrection really meant.

Rudolph Bultmann defines faith as

. . . an understanding of existence . . . Existential self-understanding can be appropriated only existentially. In my existential self-understanding, I could not learn what existence means in the abstract, but I understand in my concrete here and now, in my concrete encounters.

In answer to one of his critics, he confesses that he finds it hard to think in terms of enjoying a personal relationship with the living Christ:

I must confess . . . that the language of personal relationships with Christ is just as mythological as the other imagery you favour.

Gunther Bornkam, a disciple of Bultmann:

Certainly faith cannot and should not be dependent on the change and uncertainty of historical research.

Van Buren declares his assumptions about the nature of the universe:

If we speak of Easter as a fact, we shall have to be able to give a description of it. To take the latter tradition as a description of the appearances, however, raises far more problems than it solves. Because of the influence of the natural sciences, especially biology, on our thinking today, we can no more silence the questions concerning the changes in cells at death which spring to the mind when we read the Easter story of the Gospels, than we can deny that we live in the twentieth century.

J. S. Bezzant exposes the assumptions behind Bultmann's concept of faith, which is shared by many of these writers:

It is even said (by Bultmann) that Christ crucified and risen meets us in the word of preaching and nowhere else. Faith in the word of preaching is sufficient and absolute . . . Believe the message and it has saving efficacy. But what is the ground for believing? The answer given is Jesus' disciples' experience of the resurrection. But this is not, he holds, a historical confirmation of the crucifixion as the decisive saving event because the resurrection is also a matter of faith only, i.e. one act of faith has no other basis than another act of faith. And what is the resurrection? Another theologian who accepts the historical scepticism of Bultmann says 'the resurrection is to be understood neither as outward nor inward, neither mystically nor as a supernatural phenomenon nor as historical'. If this has any meaning it can only be that the resurrection is not to be understood in any sense. No intelligent person desires to substitute prudent acceptance of the demonstrable for faith; but when I am told that it is precisely its immunity from proof which secures the Christian proclamation from the charge of being mythological, I reply that immunity from proof can 'secure' nothing whatever except immunity from proof, and call nonsense by its proper name. Nor do I think that anything like historical Christianity can be relieved of objections by making the validity of assertions depend upon the therapeutic function it plays in healing fractures in the souls of believers, or understand how it can ever have this healing function unless it can be believed to be true.

This answer is therefore open to the same objections as the belief that the *meaning* of the resurrection can survive independently of the *event* (see pp. 96ff.). See BOOK ONE, pp. 60–73, for a further discussion of this understanding of 'faith'.

BACK TO ANSWER ONE

"It is reasonably certain that Jesus rose from the dead"

PROBLEMS AND QUESTIONS

Having examined other possible answers to the basic question, we must now return to option one, the Biblical Christian answer, and look at some of the main questions and objections raised.

 **What was the resurrection body of Jesus like?**

These are the only indications given in the accounts:

He was able to appear in a locked room (John 20: 19).

He insisted that he was not a spirit or a ghost, but that his body was tangible. The disciples therefore were able to perceive the risen Christ through three of their senses—they could see him, touch him, and hear his words. (Luke 24: 36–43).

He was recognizable by those who had known him before his death. It is true that he was not always recognized immediately (e.g. by Mary and by the disciples on the road to Emmaus). But this apparent inconsistency is understandable, since they did not expect Jesus to be raised from the dead. And if the whole story had been invented, an awkward detail like this would hardly have been included.

According to the accounts, therefore, there was some real continuity between his physical body during his lifetime and his body after the resurrection. But his resurrection body did not have all the limitations of a human body; it was not merely a resuscitated corpse.

But does the resurrection body have to be a *physical* body? Can we not believe in a *spiritual* resurrection, i.e. that Jesus survived death in a unique way, but without a visible and tangible body?

This idea runs counter to the whole way of thinking of the disciples. As Jews they would *already* have believed in a vague kind of spiritual survival beyond death in Sheol; and they would have believed in a future resurrection. But that resurrection was by definition a physicial resurrection. A purely 'spiritual' resurrection without a physical body of some kind would not have made sense to a Jew; the disciples would not have spoken of it in these terms.

We can only interpret the accounts in this way if we assume that the writers were not claiming to write accounts of what actually happened, and that they did not expect the intelligent reader to understand them literally. But this assumption is based on a particular understanding of truth, which is different from the biblical understanding. (See BOOK ONE.)

 **Don't the different accounts contradict one another?**

There are certainly some differences in the four accounts; but they hardly amount to contradictions. It does not require much ingenuity to suggest ways in which they can be fitted together. For example:

▷ *Who came to the tomb first?*

Mark 16: 1–2: 'Mary of Magdalene, and Mary the mother of James, and Salome . . . went to the tomb . . .'

Luke 23: 55: 'the women who had come with him from Galilee . . .'

Matthew 28: 1: 'Mary Magdalene and the other Mary.'

John 20: 1: 'Mary Magdalene came to the tomb . .'

These accounts would be contradictory if, and only if, they claimed to be exhaustive accounts; i.e. if John said, for example, that Mary of Magdala came *alone* to the tomb.

It is hardly reasonable to discount a report of an incident simply on the grounds that it is selective and records the incident from the point of view of *one* of those who were involved.

▷ *What did the women and the disciples see at the tomb?*

Mark 16: 5: 'a young man . . . dressed in a white robe'

Luke 24: 4: 'two men . . . in dazzling apparel'

Matthew 28: 2: 'an angel of the Lord'

John 20: 12: 'two angels in white'

This is not an insuperable difficulty if we remember that Mark and Luke were writing for a Roman audience, who might not be familiar with the idea of angels from the Old Testament.

The difference in the number of the angels would amount to a contradiction only if Mark and Matthew spoke of 'one and only one'. If one acts as spokesman for the two, we can hardly blame an eyewitness for mentioning that one only.

▷ *Why did Jesus tell Mary not to touch him, but invite Thomas to touch him?*

John 20: 17: 'Jesus said to her, "Do not hold me, for I have not yet ascended to the Father . . ."'

John 20: 27: 'Then he said to Thomas, "Put your finger here, and see my hands; and put out your hand, and place it in my side . . ."'

Mary was wanting to cling to Jesus in a physical way, and therefore Jesus had to say to her, 'Don't cling to me, because I am soon to ascend to the Father; and in this new relationship you will not be able to see me or touch me any more.' With Thomas, however, the position was different. He had said, 'Unless I see in his hands the print of the nails, and place my finger in the mark of the nails, and place my hand in his side, I will not believe' (John 20: 25). When Jesus invited Thomas to touch him, therefore, he was simply wanting to give him the firm and tangible evidence he wanted before he would believe that Jesus was alive from the dead.

If we really want to press this kind of apparent inconsistency, we are in effect saying, 'We would be more prepared to believe the documents if they agreed in every small detail.' But if the documents did agree in every small detail, would this not raise even *more* doubts in our minds and suggest that there had been some collusion amongst the writers?

And even if the documents do appear to contradict each other, what does it prove? The different accounts of an incident or of a football match show that eyewitness reports can differ enormously. But the differences only remind us that the four different people saw the event from their own standpoint. They hardly lead us to conclude that *nothing* of the kind happened. The uncertainty about some of the events surrounding the assassination of President Kennedy in 1963 only proves that we shall probably never have an exhaustive account of what happened. No one would dare to use the uncertainty to suggest that Kennedy was not assassinated.

Arnold Lunn:

Do please apply to the Resurrection narratives the same 'commonsense standards' that you would apply to any historical event. If we had two accounts of the landing of William the Conqueror we should not reject *both* because the first made him land in England with his left foot first and the second with his right foot first.

⚠️ Why doesn't Paul mention the story of the empty tomb?

In his first letter to the Corinthians, which is the earliest record of the resurrection (AD 56), Paul does not actually mention the story of the empty tomb. It is sometimes argued from this that Paul did not know the story, which must therefore be of later origin.

▷ In the passage in question—1 Corinthians 15—Paul is reminding the Corinthian Christians of the gospel he preached to them when he was with them. He is therefore simply reminding them of something they already knew, and not speaking to them as if they had never heard the story before. He introduces his summary with the words:

Now I would remind you, brethren, in what terms I preached to you the gospel . . . For I delivered to you as of first importance what I also received, that Christ died for our sins in accordance with the scriptures, that he was buried, that he was raised on the third day in accordance with the scriptures, and that he appeared to Cephas, then to the twelve. . . .

There is good reason to believe that Paul uses for his summary here an early Christian hymn or confession.

▷ The most obvious meaning of the words 'he was buried . . . he was raised on the third day' is that the body of Jesus was buried *in a tomb* and was raised *from the tomb* on the third day.

▷ Paul shows very clearly in the rest of the chapter that he believed in a physical resurrection. His understanding of the resurrection body which all men will receive was based on his understanding of the resurrection body of Jesus. He describes the resurrection body as a 'spiritual body' in the sense that it is not identical with our present physical bodies, but is immortal and imperishable.

But some one will ask, 'How are the dead raised? With what kind of body do they come?' You foolish man! What you sow does not come to life unless it dies. And what you sow is not the body which is to be, but a bare kernel, perhaps of wheat or of some other grain . . . So it is with the resurrection of the dead. What is sown is perishable, what is raised is imperishable. It is sown in dishonour, it is raised in glory. It is sown in weakness, it is raised in power. It is sown a physical body, it is raised a spiritual body . . .

For the trumpet will sound, and the dead will be raised imperishable, and we shall be changed. For this perishable nature must put on the imperishable, and this mortal nature must put on immortality . . .

Is there any evidence for the resurrection outside the New Testament?

There are several pieces of evidence from outside the New Testament which have an indirect bearing on the resurrection.

▷ *Josephus*, the Jewish historian, writing in *The Antiquities of the Jews*:

The Greek Version:

When Pilate, on the indictment of the principal men among us, had condemned him to the cross, those who loved him at the first did not cease to do so, for he appeared to them again alive on the third day . . .

The Arabic Version:

Pilate condemned him to be crucified and to die. And those who had become his disciples did not abandon his discipleship. They reported that he had appeared to them three days after his crucifixion and that he was alive.

See further p. 36.

▷ The following *inscription*, found at Nazareth, records an edict of the Emperor Claudius (AD 41–54) or the Emperor Tiberius (AD 14–37) about the robbing of graves:

Ordinance of Caesar. It is my pleasure that graves and tombs remain undisturbed in perpetuity for those who have made them for the cult of their ancestors or children or members of their house. If however any man lay information that another has either demolished them, or has in any other way extracted the buried, or has maliciously transferred them to other places in order to wrong them, or has displaced the sealing of other stones, against such a one I order that a trial be instituted, as in respect of the gods, so in regard to the cult of mortals. For it shall be much more obligatory to honour the buried. Let it be absolutely forbidden for anyone to disturb them. In case of contravention I desire that the offender be sentenced to capital punishment on charge of violation of sepulture.

Obviously we cannot be certain there is any connection between this inscription and the disappearance of the body of Jesus from the tomb. But it does suggest, at the very least, that reports had reached the Emperor about bodies being removed from tombs, perhaps in Palestine itself. This edict could possibly represent the official reaction to these reports.

▷ In 1945 the following two *inscriptions* on

ossuaries (bone-caskets) were found in a burial chamber at Talpioth, a suburb of Jerusalem. They were found by Professor E. L. Sukenik, a Jewish archaeologist, and can be dated with certainty to between AD 40 and 50.

ΙΗϹΟ ϹΙϹ

i.e. Ἰησους ἰου —which probably means 'Jesus woe!' or 'Jesus, help!' (i.e. a short prayer addressed to Jesus).

ΙΗϹ ΟΥΙ ΛΛΩΘ

i.e. Ἰησους ἀλωθ—which probably means 'Jesus, let him (who rests here) arise!'

These two inscriptions suggest that even at this early date Christians were praying to Jesus; and looking forward to a future resurrection.

▷ The *earliest Jewish writings which speak about Jesus* nowhere deny that the tomb was empty. It is reasonable to suppose that Jewish tradition would have handed down any suggestions that the tomb of Jesus had never been touched and that the body remained in the tomb. But there is no such suggestion. The Jewish traditions agreed that the tomb was empty, but explained this by saying that the disciples stole the body (this apparently despite the guard of soldiers they themselves set—Matthew 27: 62–66).

⚠ ## Didn't many religions at this time have beliefs about immortality and stories about gods rising from the dead?

▷ A belief in the survival of the individual seems to have been universal in primitive societies.

S. H. Hooke:

The archaeological evidence of primitive funerary practices shows that early man believed that his dead continued to exist in some form, and could be affected by his behaviour toward them, and could also exercise a power over him that might be either malign or benificent.

Reconstruction of an ancient burial-cave at Jericho. From earliest times pots, jars and personal effects have been buried with the dead — often for use in an after-life.

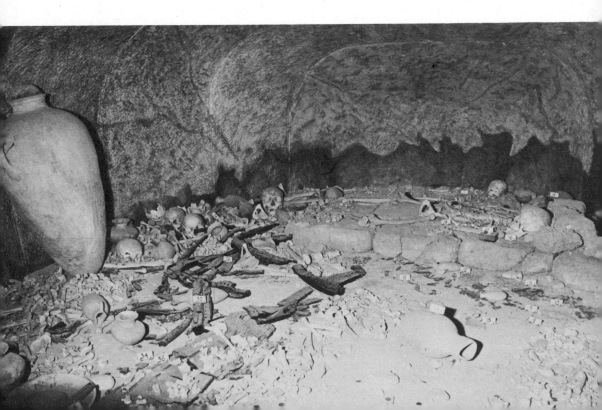

▷ The idea of resurrection is found in many of the myths of the ancient world, and is always connected with the annual cycle of agriculture (winter—death: spring—resurrection).

S. H. Hooke:

The idea of resurrection, as distinct from survival after death, or the return of the spirits or ghosts of the dead to trouble the living, appears in the mythology of both Egypt and Babylon. In Egypt we find the cult-myth of Osiris, slain and dismembered by Set, and revivified by Isis and Nepthys by means of magic spells. In Sumer and Babylon we have the myth of Tammuz, the god who dies and descends in the underworld, and is brought back to life by his sister and wife Ishtar, who descends into the under-world in search of him. Both of these myths belong to the cult pattern of an agricultural civilization. They arise out of the observation of the annual death and rebirth of vegetation, and are connected with rituals intended to secure the annual renewal of the life of nature.

▷ In these myths resurrection is only for the *gods* and not for *men*:

S. H. Hooke:

It must be remarked that in all these forms of the myth it is aways gods who die and rise again. There is no suggestion that men may share in the resurrection of the gods. This is confirmed by the Babylonian epithet for the under-world, 'the land of no-return'. There are, however, two interesting points to be noted which suggested the possibility that in some way man might share in or benefit by the death and resurrection of a god. The first is that in the Egyptian funerary cult the dead person for whom the mummification rituals are performed is thereby identified with Osiris, and his salvation in the after-life secured. The other is that in Babylonian *puhu* or substitution rituals dealing with certain forms of sickness, it was possible for the sick man to be symbolically identified with the death of Tammuz and thereby to be freed from his sickness. These faint adumbrations of what was to be developed in the pattern of revelation form part of the background of our study.

▷ The intention behind these myths and rituals was that the individual should obtain salvation; but this salvation bears little resembalance to the Christian understanding of salvation.

C. K. Barrett:

The object of the mystery cults was to secure salvation for men who were subject to moral and physical evil, dominated by Destiny, and unable by themselves to escape from the corruption that beset the material side of their nature. Salvation accordingly meant escape from Destiny, release from corruption and a renewed moral life. It was affected by what may broadly be called sacramental means. By taking part in prescribed rites the worshipper became united with God, was enabled in this life to enjoy mystical communion with him, and further was assured of immortality beyond death. This process rested upon the experiences (generally including the death and resurrection of a Saviour-God, the Lord (*kurios*)) of his devotees. The myth, which seems often to have been cultically represented, rested in many of these religions upon the fundamental annual cycle of agriculture fertility; but rites which probably were in earlier days intended to secure productiveness in field and flock were now given an individual application and effect.

▷ Against this background we can understand how, when the Christain message of the resurrection was proclaimed, some thought it ridiculous that there could be any kind of physical resurrection for the individual. But others gladly embraced the Christian gospel because it contained something *new*, and brought the fulfilment of their hopes and longings for a life with meaning and purpose beyond the grave.

⚠ Do contemporary physics and psychic research make it any easier to believe in the resurrection?

In other words do recent developments in physics and in psychic research make it easier to believe in the possibility of the resurrection of a dead man?

A. M. Ramsay:

The trend of modern science and psychology seems to have features in common which confirm the credibility of the Pauline doctrine . . . Today there is in physics the tendency to regard material objects as the organization of energy particles in particular forms, and to hold that the persistence of a body lies not in the immutability of its physical constituents but in their continual

The enigma of death and the after-life has exercised men's minds for thousands of years. Part of the Book of the Dead *written for the high priest of Amun in Egypt about 1000 BC.*

organization in accordance with the principle of the body's self-identity.

Leslie Weatherhead believes that psychic research sheds much light on the resurrection of Jesus:

Basing my summary on religious truth and what seems to me the authentic findings of psychical research, I believe that for everyone the actual experience of dying is one of great happiness, of immediate union with loved ones on the other side, and of tender, welcoming care from ministering spirits. Indeed, loved ones seem to attend the dying before death happens. Their presence has often been commented on.

The body in which we manifest ourselves immediately after death will I think *appear to us* to be still material, and indeed, may consist of highly attenuated matter on a different scale of vibration. There may be a form of 'matter' which lies between the physical as we know it and the psychical. This may account for the difficulty some newly-dead people have of realising that they are what we call 'dead'. They wonder why the living do not respond when they speak, and yet they find they can pass through closed doors. One communicator tells how 'for fun' he rushed at a door only to find he could pass right through it.

▷ In many cases, these arguments do not help a person to believe in the resurrection unless he is *already* convinced on other grounds.

David Edwards:

It would seem that this sort of scientific (or pseudo-scientific) research may help those who already believe in the resurrection of Jesus by providing foretastes and comparisons congenial to modern minds. But it gives us little or no help in answering the question: *did* Jesus rise from the dead?

▷ Sometimes, however, physics and psychic research force people to question their materialistic assumptions and to open their minds to the possibility that some phenomena cannot be explained adequately in traditional scientific terms. Then, if there is a willingness to believe that the resurrection *may* or *could* have happened, a thorough study of the evidence is still needed to show whether or not it *did* happen.

WHERE DO WE GO FROM HERE?

"Is Christianity true?"

The question we have been asking all along is simply this:

Is Christianity true?

That is, when we have discovered the basic Christian beliefs about God, man and the universe, and about Jesus Christ, do we consider that these beliefs are really true?

When we put the question as simply and baldly as this, some may see the issue as a simple choice—'Yes' or 'No.' But in fact there are other possible answers.

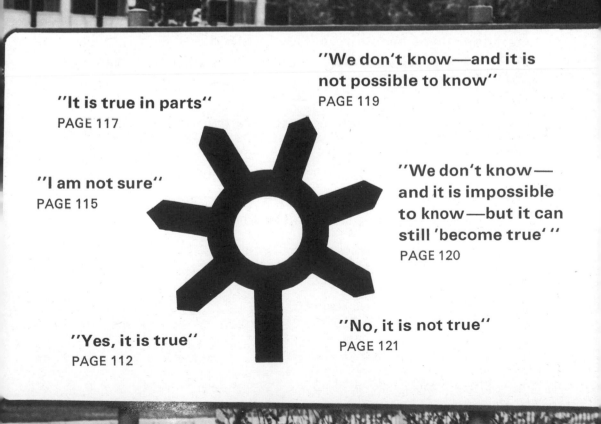

"We don't know—and it is not possible to know"
PAGE 119

"It is true in parts"
PAGE 117

"I am not sure"
PAGE 115

"We don't know—and it is impossible to know—but it can still 'become true' "
PAGE 120

"Yes, it is true"
PAGE 112

"No, it is not true"
PAGE 121

ANSWER 1

"Yes, Christianity is true"

This is to say, 'I believe—

☐ **that Christian beliefs are true in the sense that they tell us the truth about God and man and the universe (see further BOOK ONE)**

☐ **that God is personal and infinite**
the Creator of the universe and its Sustainer
loving and holy
one God and three persons;

☐ **that man is a creature created in the image of God**
and is now a rebel against God,
but capable of becoming a "son" of God;

☐ **that the universe is created and sustained by God' (see further BOOK TWO)**

'I believe—

☐ **that Christian beliefs about Jesus are true in the sense that they give us a true account of who he was and is, and of what he achieved:**

☐ **that he was both man and God, the Son of God in a unique sense;**

☐ **that he bore our sins in his death;**

☐ **that he rose from the dead and is now alive.'**

▷ The New Testament writers invite us to *believe that* certain things are true about God and about Jesus Christ:

Whoever would draw near to God must believe *that* he exists and *that* he rewards those who seek him.

If you confess with your lips *that* Jesus is Lord and believe in your heart *that* God raised him from the dead, you will be saved.

Believing that certain things are true should lead us to *believing in* Jesus Christ, and

trusting him in a personal way.

Now Jesus did many other signs in the presence of the disciples, which are not written in this book; but these are written that you may believe that Jesus is the Christ, the Son of God, and that believing you may have life in his name.

He came to his own home, and his own people received him not. But to all who received him, who believed in his name, he gave power to become children of God.

Intellectual belief and personal trust are therefore vital elements of Christian faith.

Intellectual convictions are inadequate in themselves; but without them there can hardly be a basis for a genuine personal trust.

▷ At some stage in the process of coming to faith, we need to consider exactly what it means to be a Christian. Jesus himself was very anxious that those who followed him should realize the total claims he made upon them, and that they should consider the cost carefully. At a time when large crowds were following him, he stressed the importance of counting the cost of true discipleship:

Now great multitudes accompanied him; and he turned and said to them, 'If any one comes to me and does not hate his own father and mother and wife and children and brothers and sisters, yes, and even his own life, he cannot be my disciple. Whoever does not bear his own cross and come after me, cannot be my disciple. For which of you, desiring to build a tower, does not first sit down and count the cost, whether he has enough to complete it? Otherwise, when he has laid a foundation, and is not able to finish, all who see it begin to mock him, saying, "This man began to build, and was not able to finish." Or what king, going to encounter another king in war, will not sit down first and take counsel whether he is able with ten thousand to meet him who comes against him with twenty thousand? And if not, while the other is yet a great way off, he sends an ambassy and asks terms of peace. So therefore, whoever of you does not renounce all that he has cannot be my disciple.

This means in practice that we must ask ourselves questions like these:

Am I prepared to die to myself and my own ambitions, and to put Christ first in every part of my life—my thinking and my feeling; my work, my personal relationships, my marriage, and my leisure?

Am I prepared to be identified with Christ in the eyes of others?

Am I prepared to face the same sort of treatment that he received from others—scorn, persecution, death?

Am I prepared for the sacrifice of home and comfort, wealth and reputation for the sake of sharing with Christ in working out his will among men?

Christians have gone all over the world in the service of Christ. A missionary teacher at work in Africa.

Am I prepared to be identified with other Christians, and to belong to a particular body of Christians?

While emphasizing the need to count the cost, however, Jesus also pointed out that the sacrifice involved is not a joyless or barren sacrifice:

Truly, I say to you, there is no one who has left house or brothers or sisters or mother or father or children or lands, for my sake and the gospel, who will not receive a hundredfold now in this time, houses and brothers and sisters and mothers and children and lands, with persecutions, and in the age to come eternal life.

▷ If then, I have counted the cost and want to go the whole way with Jesus, how exactly do I take the step of *becoming* a Christian? For many people, it involves a step of faith which is as simple and natural as meeting a person for the first time and establishing a friendship. They don't need to be told how to enter into a personal relationship of faith with God through Christ; when they hear the good news and believe it, they simply find themselves praying to Christ, and soon become aware that he has become a part of their lives.

For others, however, it means a more conscious process of coming to God as Creator, and of affirming a personal trust in Jesus as the Son of God who accepts us as we are and gives us the gift of the Holy Spirit.

We may take this step on our own, in secret, or with others. But sooner or later there will need to be some public profession of it—in baptism and by word of mouth.

▷ When we take the step of belief in Christ and commitment to him we receive the Holy Spirit. These are some of the things the Holy Spirit will do in us:

He will give us the inward certainty that we are now children of God:

You have received the spirit of sonship. When we cry, 'Abba! Father!' it is the Spirit himself bearing witness with our spirit that we are children of God, and if children, then heirs . . .

He will make the living Christ real to us, and help us to appreciate the extent of his love. Paul prays in these terms:

I bow my knees before the Father . . . that . . . he may grant you to be strengthened with might through his Spirit in the inner man, and that Christ may dwell in your hearts through faith; that you, being rooted and grounded in love, may have power to comprehend with all the saints what is the breadth and length and height and depth, and to know the love of Christ which surpasses knowledge, that you may be filled with all the fullness of God.

He will guide and direct us:

All who are led by the Spirit of God are sons of God.

He will work in our personality and make us more like Jesus. Paul writes about the qualities which the Spirit can produce:

The fruit of the Spirit is love, joy, peace, patience, kindness, goodness, faithfulness, gentleness, self-control . . .

He will help us to understand the teaching of Christ and the whole Bible. Jesus spoke these words to his disciples on the night of his arrest:

I have yet many things to say to you, but you cannot bear them now. When the Spirit of truth comes, he will guide you into all the truth; for he will not speak on his own authority, but whatever he hears he will speak, and he will declare to you the things that are to come. He will glorify me, for he will take what is mine and declare it to you.

▷ The Holy Spirit works within us in the context of the group of Christians or the church to which we belong. Simply by being a Christian, one belongs to the body of Christ. And this belonging is to be expressed and worked out in association with other Christians. The writer to the Hebrews urges:

Let us hold fast the confession of our hope without wavering, for he who promised is faithful; and let us consider how to stir up one another to love and good works, not neglecting to meet together, as is the habit of some, but encouraging one another, and all the more as you see the Day drawing near.

▷ This is how John describes his vision of 'a new heaven and a new earth' which is prepared for those who have trusted in Jesus Christ:

Then I saw a new heaven and a new earth; for the first heaven and the first earth had passed away, and the sea was no more. And I saw the holy city, new Jerusalem, coming down out of heaven from God, prepared as a bride adorned for her husband; and I heard a great voice from the throne saying, 'Behold, the dwelling of God is with men. He will dwell with them, and they shall be his people, and God himself will be with them; he will wipe away every tear from their eyes, and death shall be no more, neither shall there be mourning nor crying nor pain any more, for the former things have passed away.'

And he who sat upon the throne said, 'Behold, I make all things new' . . . 'To the thirsty I will give water without price from the fountain of the water of life. He who conquers shall have this heritage, and I will be his God and he shall be my son . . .'

ANSWER 2

"I am not sure"

This is to say, 'It may be true, but I am not sure. I cannot make up my mind.'

▷ Some people give this answer because they feel that they don't yet know enough about the Christian faith. And it is obvious that we cannot be pushed into believing something that we know very little about. In this case, it may simply be a problem of time. If this is how you feel, and you are in earnest, you need to be prepared to think and search until you arrive at the truth.

▷ Others give this answer because they think that this kind of presentation gives insufficient basis for any final commitment. If this is so, *how much more* would you want to know before making up your mind? Is it really the lack of evidence which makes you uncertain, or are you in fact unwilling to be convinced? Jesus himself stressed the need for this willingness:

My teaching is not mine, but his who sent me; if any man's will is to do his will (God's), he shall know whether the teaching is from God or whether I am speaking on my own authority.

This willingness to be convinced does not mean that we assume that Christianity is true and then look for reasons to confirm our assumption. It simply means that we approach all the evidence with open minds, in this frame of mind: 'I am not sure if Christianity is true. But I am prepared to consider the possibility that it *may* be true. And I am willing to believe, provided I am convinced that it is true . . . O God, if you really are there, show me the truth about

yourself, and about Jesus, and show me the truth about myself.' If you cannot approach the enquiry in this spirit, you are in virtually the same position as the person who concludes that Christianity is true only in parts (see p. 117), or that we cannot know (p. 119) or that it is not true at all (p. 121).

▷ Others give this answer because, while basically they believe, they still have many questions about Christian beliefs and about what is involved in the Christian life. But this is hardly a good enough reason for holding back. A man and a woman do not know everything about each other when they fall in love; and they do not make final detailed decisions about how to conduct their married life before they become engaged. The lesser problems of Christian belief and the details of Christian living can only be worked out in the Christian life as we live in relationship with God. Jesus understood perfectly the element of honest uncertainty in the mind of one who came to ask him to help 'if he could'; and this did not deter him from meeting his need:

Jesus said to him, 'If you can! All things are possible to him who believes.' Immediately the father of the child cried out and said, 'I believe; help my unbelief!' And . . . Jesus . . . rebuked the unclean spirit, saying to it, 'You dumb and deaf spirit, I command you, come out of him, and never enter him again.'

▷ If you give this answer because you want

to evade the challenge of Christ at this particular moment in your life, you may simply be playing for time. The Bible gives some examples of people whose procrastination prevented them from coming to know the truth.

We read of Herod:

Herod feared John, knowing that he was a righteous and holy man, and kept him safe. When he heard him, he was much perplexed; and yet he heard him gladly.

Herod knew that he was hearing the truth about himself from John the Baptist; but he lost his opportunity to hear more of the truth from him, because at a banquet he made a rash oath to Herodias' daughter, and was forced to have John beheaded.

And the king was exceedingly sorry; but because of his oaths and his guests he did not want to break his word to her.

Herod hoped that he might have another opportunity to hear the truth from Jesus himself. But Jesus was probably all too aware that Herod's curiosity would not take him any further in discovering the truth. After Pilate had examined Jesus, he passed him over to Herod:

When Herod saw Jesus, he was very glad, for he had long desired to see him, because he had heard about him, and he was hoping to see some sign done by him. So he questioned him at some length; but he made no answer.

Felix, the Roman Procurator who kept Paul in prison at Caesarea seems to have been intellectually curious about the Christian faith, but unwilling to face the moral challenge it involved for him. He hoped to postpone making a final decision; but it seems that the further opportunity never came:

He sent for Paul and heard him speak upon faith in Christ Jesus. And he argued about justice and self-control and future judgement. Felix was alarmed and said, 'Go away for the present; when I have an opportunity I will summon you.'

ANSWER 3

"It is true in parts"

This is to say, 'I accept some Christian beliefs, but not others.'
For example:

☐ I believe that there is a God, but I don't entirely accept the Bible's description of what he is like.

☐ or, I accept Christian moral teaching, Christian values and standards; but I don't believe everything that the New Testament says about Christ.

☐ or, I accept the form of words of Christian beliefs, but I don't accept the traditional interpretation of them, and feel free to reinterpret them in a different way.

▷ If you claim to be able to know for certain that some Christian beliefs are true, and some are not, what is your criterion for deciding what is true and what is false? In most cases you have to judge by the standard of reason and/or feelings. But this approach leaves you wide open to all the dangers of the answer of Rationalism and Romanticism. (See BOOK ONE, pp. 40–46.)

▷ Have you any compelling reasons for holding on to the parts of Christianity which you *do* believe to be true? You may be convinced that these beliefs are self-evident (e.g. the dignity of man), and that you can go on holding Christian values without Christian beliefs. But can you be so confident that your children and the next generation will be as easily convinced? And what do you have to say to those who go one step further than you yourself are prepared to go, and reject the *whole* system of Christian beliefs, including its values? In many cases it is little more than feeling or tradition or prejudice which makes a person hold on

to his semi-Christian beliefs and hold up his hands in horror at those who are more consistent and discard them altogether.

▷ This kind of answer is based on the assumption that Christianity is a storehouse of insights and beliefs from which we can pick and choose as we please. But Christian beliefs need to be taken together because they form a structure like a building. If you begin to take away pieces here and there, the whole structure is weakened; and if the process goes on, the building itself may well collapse.

The Sermon on the Mount gives a good example of the way in which Christian beliefs are linked with each other. It contains much straightforward moral teaching; but interwoven with this are certain claims which Jesus makes for himself:

Not every one who says to me, 'Lord, Lord,' shall enter the kingdom of heaven, but he who does the will of my Father who is in heaven. On that day many will say to me, 'Lord, Lord, did we not prophesy in your name, and cast out demons in your name, and do many mighty works in your name?' And then I will declare to them, 'I never knew you; depart from me, you evildoers.'

Similarly, in the passage in which Jesus speaks about feeding the hungry, welcoming the stranger, clothing the naked and visiting the sick, he claims that *he himself* is going to judge all men at the day of judgement according to the way in which they have acted on this teaching:

When the Son of man comes in his glory, and all the angels with him, then he will sit on his glorious throne. Before him will be gathered all the nations, and he will separate them one from another as a shepherd separates the sheep from the goats, and he will place the sheep at his right hand, but the goats at the left. Then the King will say to those at his right hand, 'Come, O blessed of my Father, inherit the kingdom prepared for you from the foundation of the world; for I was hungry and you gave me food, I was thirsty and you gave me drink . . . As you did it to one of the least of these my brethren, you did it to me.' Then he will say to those at his left hand, 'Depart from me, you cursed, into the eternal fire prepared for the devil and his angels; for I was hungry and you gave me no food, I was thirsty and you gave me no drink . . . As you did it not to one of the least of these, you did it not to me.'

If you accept *parts* of the teaching of Jesus, are you prepared for the possibility that you may come under the judgement of the *whole* of his teaching?

ANSWER 4

"We don't know— and it is not possible to know"

This is to say, 'It is impossible to know "the truth" about Christianity —or about any religion or philosophy. With our finite minds we cannot hope to know the truth about the universe as a whole. If there is any such thing as 'objective truth', it is impossible to arrive at it.

Michael Harrington, writing in *The Accidental Century:*

Once destiny was an honest game of cards which followed certain conventions, with a limited number of cards and values. Now the player realizes in amazement that the hand of his future contains cards never seen before and that the rules of the game are modified by each player.

The whole world has become a dialectical nightmare; there are no more certainties.

▷ If you give this kind of answer, no amount of 'evidence' or persuasion is likely to convince you about Christian beliefs. The discussion must turn on the implications of your agnosticism. You may *feel* and *believe* in this total uncertainty; but do you, or can

you *live* permanently with it? The more consistently you live with your belief in total uncertainty, the more intolerable your present life will be. (See further, BOOK ONE, pp. 47–59.)

▷ If your total uncertainty is not justified, and if Christianity is true, the despair of being finally rejected by God will be even more profound than the despair of living in a world without any certainties.

▷ In practice, you are living as if Christianity is *not true*. It is not that you still have an open mind and are prepared to accept the possibility that it might really be true. You are in effect acting on the assumption that it is *not true*. (See pp. 121 ff.).

ANSWER 5

"We don't know—and it is impossible to know—but it can still 'become true'"

This is to say, 'We can never hope to know for certain if Christianity is true; but it can still be "true for me" in my own experience.'

Wilfred Cantwell Smith:

Religions are not propositions and therefore cannot be true and false in that particular sense of those terms. However, this is not the only sense in which truth is to be conceived. The propositional notion of truth and falsehood, as attributes of statements, has tended to dominate Western thought since the Enlightenment. The re-awakening, however, of our awareness that faith is not a belief in theories, that God has given to us for our salvation not a doctrinal system, should have alerted us more effectively than has sometimes been the case, to a deeper understanding also of truth itself . . . Impersonal truth perhaps lends itself to statement form, but personal truth appears in another quality.

The religion of one Christian may be more true, or more false, at a given moment than at another moment, or than the religion of another Christian . . . The religion of one Muslim may be more true, or more false, at a given moment than at another moment, or than the religion of another Muslim. This must be conceded, must be grasped in all its terrifying and its life-giving quality.

Once it is grasped, a vital issue follows. The question of serious significance then becomes: may the religion of a particular Christian be more true, and may it be more false, than the religion of a particular Muslim?

Rather than what is in general, religious truth is, I suggest, a matter of what is in actuality; and therefore, also, of what has been, and what will be. The future religious history of mankind is open.

Even those who like to think that religions have been false in the past, should hope that they will become true in the future.

This answer is more than a protest against a purely intellectual assent to Christian beliefs, and it falls far short of genuine Christian faith. It denies the possibility of being able to give any genuine intellectual assent, and asserts that the *only* real kind of truth is the truth of experience.

This kind of answer is becoming more and more popular today; but it presents perhaps the most serious and the most subtle challenge to historic Christianity. It suffers from the weaknesses of the agnosticism on which it is based (see BOOK ONE, pp. 47–59) and of the Existentialist and Mystic answers to the question of truth. (see BOOK ONE, pp. 60–73 and pp. 74–78.)

ANSWER 6

"No, it is not true"

This is to say, 'Christian beliefs about God, man and the universe are not true. Jesus was not the Son of God; his death has no special meaning, and he did not rise from the dead. The whole of Christianity, its moral values and its way of life must also be rejected; for since the foundation (i.e. the beliefs about God and about Jesus) is not true, what is built on that foundation (i.e. the moral teaching) cannot be true either.'

▷ This answer does at least assume that some things are true and some are not. And it is therefore closer to the Christian understanding of truth than the answer which says that Christianity is neither true nor false, or that it is impossible to know for certain. It means that we can at least still talk in terms of verification and falsification. (see BOOK ONE, pp. 13–30.)

▷ Sometimes this answer is based entirely on the impression made by the lives of Christians in the past or the present. For some, the verdict is simple and clear-cut.

Lord Boothby:

The history of the Christian churches has been one of such atrocious cruelty. All of them have done untold harm to the world . . . The traditions of the Christian churches, for centuries, can be summarized as 'Dogma, persecution, secession, hatred, destruction and fire.' In fact, everything that Jesus loathed and denounced.

A person who is examining Christianity has every right to look at the record of the Christian church to see if it bears out the truth of Christian beliefs, just as a person examining the claims of Communism should

look at the record of Communist countries. But many people think that when they have

British politician, Lord Boothby.

discovered something doubtful or discreditable in the church's record in the past or the present, they can safely reject the whole of Christianity as untrue. The danger in this approach is that our interpretation of the record of the church is bound to be influenced by the assumptions with which we approach the subject. The Christian therefore has to say: 'You have every right to look at us to see if our lives produce any evidence to suggest that what we believe is true. But at the same time, remember that we don't claim to be perfect, and we are ashamed of many of the things which have been done in the name of Christ. If Christianity is true, you will be judged in the end not by what you think of the Christian church, but by what you think of your Creator and of Jesus Christ.'

Even those who oppose Christianity would be prepared to concede that not everyone who claims to be a Christian is a Christian at heart. In some societies there has been a Christian consensus and everyone has been regarded as a Christian, at least in name. But this has never meant that each individual was fully convinced of Christian beliefs or fully committed to live in obedience to Christ. Jesus said, 'By their fruits ye shall know them.' And if a person's behaviour is far from Christian, we have good reason to doubt the genuineness of his Christianity.

The fact that perversions of Christianity exist is not necessarily an adequate reason for rejecting Christian beliefs. In his corespondence with Arnold Lunn, C. E. M. Joad cannot refrain from ridiculing things that Christians have done and said. This is Arnold Lunn's reply:

It is pleasant to remain young, and I am impressed by the boyish glee with which you collect newspaper cuttings to show up Christianity in a bad light. The love of God is a fine emotion and, like all fine emotions, capable of being degraded and vulgarised. It would be just as easy to ridicule human love by a collection of extracts from cheap novelists as to expose the love of God with the aid of your religious scrap book. As easy, and as futile.

Granting that perversions exist, and that much harm has been done in the name of Christ, is there any religion or philosophy which has a similar record of solid, lasting good?

▷ If you believe that Christianity is not true,

this does not mean that there is no more that the Christian can say. There are still many areas open for discussion even when there is no agreement about God and about Jesus Christ. We can continue to talk about man and about our common experience of what it means to be human. In this discussion the Christian, provided he has really listened and understood what the issues are, is entitled to press gently but firmly by asking questions such as these:

How far are you prepared to go with others who have tried to be consistent and have taken this rejection to its logical conclusion?

Nietzsche:

Vast upheavals will happen in the future, as soon as men realise that the structure of Christianity is only based on assumptions . . . I have tried to deny everything.

Jean-Paul Sartre:

Atheism is a cruel, long-term business; I believe I have gone through it to the end.

If you dislike or disagree with the conclusions which men like these have arrived at, where do you think they have gone wrong? You may feel at many points that although you share the same *starting-point*, you do not agree with the *conclusions* at which they have arrived. There are bound to be differences in the conclusions, and differences in the degrees of consistency with which they are lived out. But if these are possible conclusions which follow from the initial assumptions, what is there that prevents you from following the same road and accepting the same conclusion? Can you appeal to some firm principle to show why the conclusion is wrong or unnecessary? Or do you hold back because you are relying simply on habit, or the force of tradition, or a consensus of opinion, or 'common sense' or pure sentiment?

Can you in practice be thoroughly consistent in your belief and at the same time live in the world as it is?

Many writers who are not Christians are very well aware of the problem of living with their beliefs.

David Hume:

Thus the sceptic still continues to reason and

believe, though he asserts that he cannot defend his reason by reason, and by the same rule, he must assent to the principle concerning the existence of the body, though he cannot pretend by any argument of philosophy to maintain its veracity.

Kathleen Knott, writing about Hume's inconsistency:

Among great philosophers, Hume, who hung his nose as far as any over the nihilistic abyss, withdrew it sharply when he saw the psychological risks involved and advised dilution of metaphysics by playing backgammon and making merry with his friends. The conclusion of Hume's philosophising was indeed a radical scepticism, which left no convincing logical grounds for believing anything natural, let alone supernatural, was there at all, and he saved his 'reason' or, as we might say, his 'philosophical personality' . . . by refusing to take the implications of his philosophy to heart.

Paul Hazard, writing about the sceptics of the eighteenth century:

Peculiar people, psychologically, these scholars. They will set a fuse to the most daring ideas, apparently unaware or regardless of what they are doing. It is their successors who, in the fulness of time, realise the implications of their legacy. Meanwhile, they themselves still cling to tradition.

H. J. Blackham, writing about Nietzsche:

His thinking was ancillary to the real philosophic task he set himself of experimentally *living* all the valuations of the past, together with the contraries, in order to acquire the right to judge them . . . There are positions which can be thought but not lived, there are exploratory ventures from which there is no return. Nietzsche's thoughts were fascinated by unexplored forbidden regions of abysses, glaciers, and mountain peaks. One can look down into the bottom of an abyss refusing the possibility of throwing oneself over the edge, but one cannot explore the possibility by a tentative jump. One can examine in thought the possibility of nihilism (as an irresolvable conflict between human valuations and cosmic facts) and try to show that it is not the truth; but if one is determined to will and to live the possibility of nihilism, then one no longer has any independent standpoint under one's feet; worse than Kierkegaard 'out upon the seventy thousand fathoms of water', one is actually sucked down and engulfed: what from the independent standpoint of responsible freedom was regarded as the unavoidable ambiguity of

good and evil in the world becomes, first, the ambiguity of one's own will, and then its abandonment to the eternal destruction and the eternal return and the dionysian ecstasy. No more than scepticism can be overcome by doubting it can nihilism be overcome by willing it.

Albert Camus:

What matters . . . is not to follow things back to their origins, but, the world being what it is, to know how to live in it.

Lazare Bickel:

Intelligence is our faculty for not developing what we think to the very end, so that we can still believe in reality.

These different kinds of inconsistency are what *Francis Schaeffer* describes as the 'point of tension'—the tension being between the logical conclusions of a person's belief and the direction in which the real world draws him. The Christian therefore feels that he must seek to expose the hidden defences which prevent a person from feeling the keenness of his inconsistency.

At the point of tension the person is not in a place of consistency in his system and the roof is built *as a protection against the blows of the real world*, both internal and external. It is like the great shelters built upon some mountain passes to protect vehicles from the avalanches of rock and stone which periodically tumble down the mountain. The avalanche, in the case of the non-Christian, is the real and the abnormal fallen world which surrounds him. The Christian, lovingly and with true tears, must remove the shelter and allow the truth of the external world and of what man is to beat upon him. When the roof is off, each man must stand naked and wounded before the truth of what is.

The truth that we let in first is not a dogmatic statement of the truth of the Scriptures but the truth of the external world and the truth of what man himself is. This is what shows him his need. The Scriptures then show him the nature of his lostness and the answer to it.

Is it possible that your rejection of Christian beliefs is based on personal rather than intellectual reasons?
The Christian has no right to assume that *all* intellectual problems are a kind of smokescreen and therefore do not deserve a thorough and honest answer. He is putting a real stumbling-block in the way of many doubters and questioners if he tries to reduce every

intellectual question to a moral question.

At the same time, however, the Gospels show that *some* people refused to become followers of Christ, not because they were unconvinced in their minds, but because they considered the cost too great in practical terms:

The *rich young ruler* refused to follow Jesus because he was so attached to his wealth:

And Jesus looking upon him loved him, and said to him, 'You lack one thing; go, sell what you have, and give to the poor, and you will have treasure in heaven; and come, follow me.' At that saying his countenance fell, and he went away sorrowful; for he had great possessions.

Jesus told the parable of the *banquet* to pin-point certain excuses to do with business, other interests, and the family:

They all alike began to make excuses. The first said to him, 'I have bought a field, and I must go out and see it; I pray you, have me excused.' And another said, 'I have bought five yoke of oxen, and I go to examine them; I pray you, have me excused.' And another said, 'I have married a wife, and therefore I cannot come.'

The *Pharisees* would not commit themselves because of the effect it would have on their reputation. Jesus said to them:

How can you believe, who receive glory from one another and do not seek the glory that comes from the only God?

Are you willing to think again, and to reconsider the Christian answers with an open mind, and if necessary admit that you have been wrong?

Aldous Huxley, writing about his earlier beliefs:

It was the manifestly poisonous nature of the fruits that forced me to consider the philosophical tree on which they had grown.

An obviously untrue philosophy of life leads in practice to disastrous results.

He speaks about

. . the point where we realize the necessity of seeking an alternative philosophy that shall be true and therefore fruitful of good.

The Christian is bound to feel that Huxley's

earlier dissatisfaction with his position never led him to consider Christian faith as such an 'alternative philosophy' which would be true and therefore 'fruitful of good'. He will want to point to the 'poisonous nature' of Huxley's later position. But the method he outlines here of seeking an alternative answer goes some way towards explaining what repentance means.

C. E. M. Joad thought again, and it eventually led him to Christian faith. His correspondence with Arnold Lunn, published first in 1932, was carried out on the assumption that it is possible and essential to find out 'the truth' about Christianity. He was at least willing to be convinced. And in 1942, in a new preface to the correspondence, he wrote about the way in which he had been forced to think again and change some of his ideas:

For some years . . . my own views have been insensibly changing, and the change has reflected, indeed it has been occasioned by the deepening tragedy of the contemporaty world.

When he later abandoned his agnosticism and became a Christian, he wrote the following words about his change of mind:

There is such a thing as the pride of the intellect, a pride in which throughout my life I have been continuously proud. There are certain writers—Shaw is one of them, Swift another and Bertrand Russell another—from whom I derive an enormous intellectual stimulation. Borne aloft on the wings of their intellects, I feel myself raised to an eminence from which I look down upon the past and the present of my species, and, as momentarily I perceive through Shaw's eyes or through Russell's, I observe, with amused detachment, its manifold follies, follies from which, while the moment of exaltation lasts, I fondly believe myself exempt. I am suffused with a feeling of immense superiority, as I thank God that I am not as other men.

If it turns out that Christianity is true, and you have rejected it—what then? What you are doing amounts to this: you are rejecting the God who has made you and the universe, the God who has given you your body and mind and feelings, and is the source of everything you enjoy. You are not simply rejecting one of the great world religions, or a particular outlook on life. You are saying 'No!' to your Creator, and 'No!' to the one who came to reveal the Creator more fully and

Albrecht Durer's illustration of John's vision of the glorified Jesus in Revelation 1. God has given Christ power and authority to rule and judge the world.

to reconcile you to him.

You will not be able to claim in the end, 'I had no opportunity to find out the truth. I had no convincing clues to point to the truth.' You will be held responsible for your choice, because you rejected the clear indications you had, however small they were—in the universe, in your conscience, in the Bible and in Jesus.

Are you prepared to accept the consequences of your choice, here in this life and in the life beyond death? When we have made every allowance for the metaphorical language of Jesus and other writers in the New Testament, we must realize that this language is meant to describe as honestly and clearly as possible the despair and agony of being cut off from God—a despair which is deeper than any despair we can know in this life:

Then the kings of the earth and the great men and the generals and the rich and the strong, and every one, slave and free, hid in the caves and among the rocks of the mountains, calling to the mountains and the rocks, 'Fall on us and hide us from the face of him who is seated on the throne, and from the wrath of the Lamb; for the great day of their wrath has come, and who can stand before it?'

These warnings of judgement are not intended by the writers as cruel threats to compel a terrified and blind surrender. They are rather urgent appeals, in the light of what is to happen, to think again about the truth.

For God so loved the world that he gave his only Son, that whoever believes in him should not perish but have eternal life. For God sent the Son into the world, not to condemn the world, but that the world might be saved through him. He who believes in him is not condemned; he who does not believe is condemned already, because he has not believed in the name of the only Son of God. And this is the judgement, that the light has come into the world, and men loved darkness rather than light, because their deeds were evil. For everyone who does evil hates the light, and does not come to the light, lest his deeds should be exposed. But he who does what is true comes to the light, that it may be clearly seen that his deeds have been wrought in God.

In this enquiry, we have been putting Christianity 'on trial'. But if Christianity is true, *I* am the one who is on trial. The issues are clear-cut; and how each one of us responds to the love of God is a matter of life and death.

REFERENCES

PAGES 9–19
Matthew 1:18–25; Luke 1:26–35; Mark 6:32–34
Mark 10:13–16; 1:40–42; Luke 7:12–15; 15:1–2; Mark 7:6,8,9; Matthew 23:13, 16–17, 25, 28
Mark 11:15–17; John 11:33–36; 5:30; 6:38; Luke 22:24–27; John 13:3–5, 12–15; Mark 7:37; John 8:46; 1 Peter 2:22; 1 John 1:8; 3:5; Mark 13:32; Matthew 11:27; 12:50; 16:27; John 10:30; 5:22–23
John 14:6–7; Mark 1:15; 10:45; 14:24; 14:61–62; Luke 4:18–21; 24:44, 46; John 5:39; 5:46; Mark 2:5–10; John 5:21; 11:25; Matthew 5:21–22; Mark 13:31; John 18:37; Matthew 25:31–32
John 5:22–23; Matthew 11:28–29; Luke 14:26; John 7:37; 6:29; 14:1; Matthew 20:29–34
Mark 8:1–2; Matthew 15:31; Mark 2:8–12; Matthew 11:2–5; John 10:37–38; Mark 8:11–13
Hebrews 2:14; 4:15; James 2:1; 1 Corinthians 15:47; Philippians 2:6–11
John 1:18; 1 John 1:1–3; Romans 5:12–19; 1 Corinthians 5:18–19; 1 Timothy 2:5–6
Hebrews 2:17–18; 4:15; John 17:20–26

PAGE 20
The Truth Shall Make You Free, Watchtower Society, pp. 248–250

PAGES 21–22
John 14:28; 10:30; 14:9–10; Philippians 2:5–7; Luke 18:19
Luke 18:22; Colossians 1:15ff.
C. F. D. Moule, *Colossians and Philemon*, Cambridge New Testament Commentary, CUP 1957, p. 64
Hebrews 1:1–4
The Truth Shall Make You Free, p. 254

PAGE 23
H. Danby, *The Jew and Christianity*, Sheldon Press 1927, pp.8–9
The Jewish Encyclopedia, Vol. VII, pp. 161, 163

PAGE 24
The Jewish Encyclopedia, Vol. VII, pp. 163–164, 162

PAGE 25
Claude Montefiore; in Herbert Danby, *The Jew and Christianity*, p.79
Sholem Asch, *My Personal Faith*, Routledge 1942, pp. 106–107
Herbert Danby, *The Jew and Christianity*, p. 23

PAGE 26
The Jewish Encyclopedia, Vol. VII, p. 166
The Koran, tr. N. J. Dawood, Penguin 1964, Sura 19:19–22, p. 33; 3:42, p. 398
Tradition; in M. Goldsack, *Christ in Islam*, Christian Literature Society of India 1905, p. 32

PAGE 27
Sura 4:169, p. 371
Traditions; in M. Goldsack, *Christ in Islam*, pp. 25, 41
Sura 5:112–115, p. 386; 19:26–31, pp. 33–34; 5:112–115, pp. 386–387; 5:110–111, p. 386

PAGE 28
Henri Michaud, *Jésu selon le Coran*, p. 10; in Geoffrey Parrinder, *Jesus in the Qur'an*, Faber 1965, p. 166

PAGE 29
Sura 5:116, p. 387; 6:101, p. 421; 23:91, p. 218; 5:72–75, pp. 382–383

PAGE 30
Hugh Schonfield, *The Passover Plot*, Hutchinson 1965, pp. 10–11
Paul van Buren, *The Secular Meaning of the Gospel*, Penguin, pp. 126–127

PAGE 31
Hugh Schonfield, *The Passover Plot*, pp. 9–10

PAGE 32
Joel Carmichael, *The Death of Jesus* Penguin, pp. 8, 10
Paul van Buren, *The Secular Meaning of the Gospel*, pp. 16, 30

PAGE 33
F. C. Happold, *Religious Faith and Twentieth Century Man*, Penguin 1966, p. 150
John Robinson, *Honest to God*, SCMPress 1963, pp. 72–76

PAGE 34
F. C. Happold, *Religious Faith and Twentieth Century Man*, pp. 145, 124, 52–53
John Robinson, *Honest to God*, pp. 67, 68

PAGE 35
Pliny; in *Documents of the Christian Church*, ed. Henry Bettinson,
OUP 1946, pp. 3–5
Tacitus; in the same, p. 2
Suetonius; in the same, p. 3

PAGE 36
Josephus; Professor Shlomo Pines, in *Journal of Israeli Academy of Science and Humanities*, 1973; quoted by Peter-Allen Frost, *Church of England Newspaper*, August 1973

PAGE 37
Josephus, *Antiquities of the Jews;* in Roderic Dunkerley, *Beyond the Gospels*, Penguin 1957, p. 34
Roderic Dunkerly, *Beyond the Gospels*, pp. 29–30

PAGE 38
Luke 2:18–19; 2:51; John 8:41; Galatians 4:4
Nicholas Zernov, *Eastern Christendom*, A Study of the Origin and Development of the Eastern Orthodox Church, Weidenfeld and Nicholson 1961, p. 234

PAGES 39–40
Luke 1:28, 30–31; 1:38; Mark 3:31–35; Luke 11:27–28; John 2:4; 19:26–27
Acts 1:14
The Jewish Encyclopedia, Vol. VII, p. 161
Mark 6:2–3; Galatians 1:19
Roderic Dunkerley, *Beyond the Gospels*, pp. 97–98

PAGES 41–44
1 John 1:1; Psalm 53:2–3; Isaiah 53:6; 1 Peter 2:21–23; 1 John 3:5; Mark 2:7; 2:16; 2:18; 2:24
Mark 3:11–12; 8:29-30; 11:27–33
Mark 8:29–31; 9:9–10; Matthew 26:63–65
Mark 3:5–6; John 2:11; 4:53; 5:18; 6:1–15; 6:1–71; 9:34–39; 11:45–53
The Gospel of Thomas; in *The Apocryphal New Testament*, tr. M. R. James, OUP 1924, pp. 62–63

PAGES 45–48
Genesis 1:26; 5:1–3; Daniel 7:13–14
Job 38:4–7; Hosea 11:1; 2 Samuel 7:8–14; 1 John 3:1–3
Matthew 11:25–27; John 8:55
Proverbs 3:1; 4:1–4; John 5:19–20
Thomas Boslooper, *The Virgin Birth*, SCM Press 1962, p. 186
Professor Zaehner; in H. D. Lewis, *The Study of Religions*, Penguin, p. 145

PAGES 49–62
Hosea 11:1–4; Deuteronomy 8:1, 6, 11, 19–20
Exodus 34:6–7; Jeremiah 5:7–9; Ezekiel 18:23; Genesis 2:16–17; Romans 5:12; 6:23; James 1:15
Numbers 30:15; Leviticus 10:17; 16:22; Isaiah 53:5–6; 53:11; 53:12; 53:10
Leviticus 24:15–16; Deuteronomy 21:22–23; Mark 8:31–32; 9:30–31; 10:32–34; 14:6–10; 14:22–25
Matthew 26:39; 26:42; Psalm 75:8; Jeremiah 25:15–16; Isaiah 51:17; Mark 14:32–36; 15:2–15
John 18:38; Luke 23:15; 23:41; 23:47; 23:33–34; John 19:26–27; Luke 23:42–43; Mark 15:34; Luke 23:46; John 19:28–30
John 1:29; 1 John 2:1–2; Luke 24:46–47; 1 Peter 2:24; 3:18; 1 Corinthians 15:3; Hebrews 1:3; Colossians 2:13–14
Romans 5:8–9; 1 John 4:10, Revised Version; Romans 6:10; 6:23; Hebrews 10:12–14, 18; Galatians 3:13; Luke 24:45–47; Exodus 12:11–13; Deuteronomy 16:1–3
1 Corinthians 5:7; 1 Peter 1:18–19; Romans 8:1–3; John 18:11; Romans 5:1, 8–9; 1 Peter 1:18
Colossians 2:13–15; Romans 5:8, 10–11; 5:9; 1 Peter 2:21–23
1 Peter 4:13; Luke 9:23–26; Philippians 3:7–10; 2 Corinthians 5:14–15; Philippians 2:5–8; 1 Corinthians 8:11; 2 Corinthians 1:3–7; 1 Corinthians 15:56–57; Philippians 1:21; Revelation 12:10–12

PAGE 63
J. W. C. Wand, *The Atonement*, SPCK 1963, p. 12
David Edwards, *God's Cross in Our World*, SCM Press 1963, p. 41

PAGES 64 and 67
John 3:16; 1 John 4:8–18; Romans 5:8–9; 1 Peter 2:20–24
Hebrews 10:12–14; 1 Peter 1:18–21

PAGE 68
Rudolph Bultmann, *Kerygma and Myth*, ed. H. W. Bartsch, Vol. I, SCM Press, pp. 36–39
Colin Wilson, *Religion and the Rebel*, Gollancz 1957, p. 29
Dietrich Bonhoeffer, *Letters and Papers from Prison*, Collins Fontana 1959, p. 164

PAGE 69
Paul van Buren, *The Secular Meaning of the Gospel*, pp. 154–155
David Edwards, *God's Cross in Our World*, pp. 37ff.
Nikos Kazantzakis, *Christ Recrucified*, Faber 1968, pp. 466–467

Thomas Mann; quoted on the cover of Kazantzakis, *Christ Recrucified*

PAGE 70
F. C. Happold, *Religious Faith and Twentieth Century Man*, p. 172
C. E. M. Joad, *Is Christianity True?*, pp. 72–73
J. Gresham Machen, *Christianity and Liberalism*, Victory Press 1923, pp. 120–121

PAGE 71
Rudolph Bultmann, *Kerygma and Myth*, Vol. I, pp. 7–8
John Robinson, *Honest to God*, p. 78

PAGE 72
The Jewish Encyclopedia, Vol. VII, p. 166
Tacitus; in *Documents of the Christian Church*, p. 2
Talmud; in Roderic Dunkerley, *Beyond the Gospels*, p. 50

PAGE 73
Mark 10:45; 15:37–38; 1 Peter 3:18; 2:24

PAGE 75
Lin Yutang; in *What I Believe*, Allen and Unwin 1966, p. 80
A. J. Ayer; in *I Believe*, Allen and Unwin,p. 16
Albert Camus; in Camus, *A Collection of Critical Essays*, ed. Germaine Brée, Spectrum 1965, p. 68
Luke 1:76
J. C. Pollock, *Moody Without Sankey*, Hodder and Stoughton, p. 73

PAGE 76
Kenneth Barnes, in *What I Believe*

PAGE 77
B. B. Warfield, 'Modern Theories of the Atonement,' in *The Person and Work of Christ*, Presbyterian and Reformed Publishing Co. 1950, p. 386

PAGE 79
Genesis 2:16–17; Exodus 21:15–16; 21:22–25; Luke 19:41–44
Leon Morris, *Glory in the Cross*, Hodder and Stoughton 1966, pp. 76–77

PAGE 80–82
Lord Byron; in Basil Willey, *Nineteenth Century Studies*, Chatto and Windus 1949, p. 75
Acts 20:28
2 Corinthians 5:19; Romans 5:12, 15–17; 5:18–19; Hebrews 9:26; 10:12, 14; Romans 5:1–2
Matthew 16:22
The Jewish Encyclopedia, Vol. VII, p. 167
Hans Joachim Schoeps, *The Jewish Christian Argument*, Faber 1965, p. 23
Matthew 16:23, New English Bible; John 12:27
Matthew 26:52–54; Luke 24:25–27; 24:45–47

PAGE 83
Sura 4:156–157, p. 370
Kenneth Cragg; in M. Kamel Hussein, *City of Wrong*, tr. Kenneth Cragg, Djambatan (Amsterdam) 1959, pp. x–xi
Hebrews 2:14–15

PAGES 86–91
Acts 1:3, New English Bible
Acts 2:32, 36; Luke 24:44–47; Ephesians 2:18; Hebrews 7:25; Romans 6:4–11
Philippians 3:8–11; Romans 14:7–9; 2 Corinthians 1:8–10; 2 Timothy 1:10; 1 Peter 1:3; Hebrews 2:14–15; 1 Corinthians 15:51–55

PAGE 96
The Jewish Encyclopedia, Vol. IV, p. 51
Hugh Schonfield, *The Passover Plot*, p. 7

PAGE 97
Ronald Gregor Smith, *Secular Christianity*, Collins 1966, p. 103
Hugh Sconfield, *The Passover Plot*, pp. 172, 180

PAGE 98
Lewis Carroll, *Alice in Wonderland*, Macmillan 1966, p. 60

PAGE 99
David Hume, *An Enquiry Concerning Human Understanding*, Section X, Of Miracles, Collins Fontana, pp. 210–212, 222–223
C. S. Lewis, *Miracles*, Bles 1947, pp. 122–123

PAGE 100
C. E. M. Joad, *Is Christianity True?*, pp. 269–270

PAGE 102
Rudolph Bultmann, *Kerygma and Myth*, Vol. I, pp. 42–43
Harvey Cox, 'A Dialogue on Christ's Resurrection'; in *Christianity Today*, 12 April 1968, p. 9

PAGE 103
Paul van Buren, *The Secular Meaning of the Gospel*, pp. 132–133
John Wren-Lewis, *I Believe*, p. 236
John Wren-Lewis, 'Does Science Destroy Belief?'; in *Fact, Faith and Fantasy*, Collins Fontana 1964, p. 43
Eduard Schweitzer, *Jesus*, SCM Press 1971, pp. 49–51

PAGE 104
Rudolph Bultmann, *Kerygma and Myth*, Vol. I
Gunther Bornkam; in Colin Brown, *Philosophy and Christian Faith*, Tyndale Press 1969
Paul van Buren; *The Secular Meaning of the Gospel*
J. S. Bezzant/; in *Objections to Christain Belief*, Constable 1963, pp. 90–91

PAGE 106
Arnold Lunn, *Is Christianity True?*, p. 259

PAGE 107
1 Corinthians 15:1–5; 15:35–37, 42:44, 52–53
Josephus; see under p. 36
Ordinance of Claudius; in *The New Testament Background, Selected Documents*, C. K. Barrett, SPCK 1961, p. 15

PAGE 108
E. L. Sukenik; in Berndt Gustafson, *New Testament Studies*, 1956, pp. 65–66
S. H. Hooke, *The Resurrection of Christ*, Darton, Longman and Todd 1967, p. 1

PAGE 109
S. H. Hooke, *The Resurrection of Christ*, pp. 2–3
C. K. Barrett, *The New Testament Background*, pp. 92–93
A. M. Ramsay, *The Resurrection of Christ*, Bles 1945, p. 112

PAGE 110
Leslie Weatherhead, *The Christian Agnostic*, Hodder and Stoughton 1965, p. 238
David Edwards, *God's Cross in Our World*, p. 144

PAGES 112–118
Hebrews 11:6; Romans 10:9; John 20:30–31; 1:11–12
Luke 14:25–33; Mark 10:29–30
Romans 8:15–16; Ephesians 3:14–19; Romans 8:14; Galatians 5:22; John 16:12–14; Hebrews 10:23–25; Revelation 21:1–7
John 7:16–17; Mark 9:23–25
Mark 6:20; 6:26; Luke 23:8–9; Acts 24:24–27
Matthew 7:21–23; 25:31–46

PAGE 119
Michael Harrington, *The Accidental Century*, Penguin, p. 11

PAGE 120
Wilfred Cantwell Smith, *Questions of Religious Truth*, pp. 68–69

PAGE 121
Lord Boothby, *I Believe*, p. 4
Arnold Lunn, *Is Christianity True?*
Nietzsche; in Colin Wilson, *The Outsider*, p. 133
Jean-Paul Sartre, *Words*, tr. Irene Clephane, Penguin 1964, p. 157
David Hume, *Treatise on Human Nature*, I. IV. I

PAGE 123
Kathleen Knott, *Objections to Humanism*, Penguin 1967, p. 62
Paul Hazard, *The European Mind in the Eighteenth Century*, p. 82
H. J. Blackham, *Six Existentialist Thinkers*, Routledge 1965, p. 41
Albert Camus, *The Rebel*, tr. Anthony Bower, Penguin 1967, p. 12
Lazare Bickel; in Camus, *The Rebel*, pp. 258–259
Francis Schaeffer, *The God who is There*, Hodder and Stoughton 1968, p. 129

PAGE 124
Mark 10:21–22; Luke 14:18–20; John 5:44
Aldous Huxley, *Ends and Means*, Chatto and Windus 1937, pp. 275, 284
C. E. M. Joad, *Is Christianity True?*, introduction
C. E. M. Joad, *Recovery of Belief*, Faber 1952, p. 28

PAGE 125
Revelation 6:15–17; John 3:16–21

INDEX